AUSTRALIA

History of Australia

Discover the Major Events that
Shaped the History of Australia

DINGO
BOOK CLUB

www.dingopublishing.com

"Great Books Change Life"

Table of Contents

Introduction

Although Australia may appear as a hostile, arid chunk of land at first glance, the truth is that this mystical, faraway land is rich in more ways than one. Apart from kangaroos and other iconic, endemic species that roam the Australian landscape, the Land Down Under is also home to a vibrant and diverse culture, as well as some of the oldest surviving folk traditions maintained by Aboriginal Australians. Being incredibly diverse themselves, the indigenous people of Australia are made up of a wide range of tribes that speak many languages and maintain countless ancient customs.

Genetic and cultural research has confirmed that many of the Aborigines can indeed trace their origins back to the first people that came to Australia, which would make them the oldest population on Earth. As we embark on the great journey that is the Australian story, you will learn, in detail, just how fascinating this long history is. Thanks to the many endemic Australian species that are found both in the flora and fauna, as well as the longevity of existing, indigenous human communities, the deceivingly barren country of Australia is an object of much interest among biologists and anthropologists alike.

Australia's colonial era has no shortage of stories to tell either, ranging from misconceptions to landmark historical events that left an everlasting impact and shaped the country as we know it today. Both the early explorers and the consolidators of the modern Australian society have left tremendous marks, yet many people still don't know much about this period, and they harbor quite a few wrong ideas about that time. For generations, both in Australia and in many other parts of the western world, students were taught incorrect information that the first settlers in Australia were the British.

While the British certainly played a decisive role in Australia's development, they weren't quite the first to arrive, which is just one of the misconceptions that are all too common. How and when the Dutch got there first will become abundantly clear in the early chapters of this book where we will delve deeper into these defining historical events.

As we proceed through the chapters, we will explore the entire journey that Australia has had to make to arrive at the point where it is today. Like many other former colonies, Australia gives off the illusion of having a short and uneventful past, which could not be further from the truth. Apart from the indigenous people and their stories, even the relatively brief colonial period is enough of a tale to fill out several volumes. This book aims to put that information and more into a comprehensive and accessible read for all of those who wish to acquaint themselves with this unique country.

In addition to history, we will also delve into the life and structure of contemporary Australian society and state. This will provide insight into what exactly it means to be Australian and how the country's past has defined this modern, developed land, which 25 million people now call their home. You will find that, as always, there is more than meets the eye, and that Australia not only has a rich history but has also contributed a great deal to the world as a whole.

Chapter 1: Aboriginal People

Australian Indigenous Culture

When the first Europeans arrived in Australia, they ignored the culture and people they found there to a large extent. This attitude has tended to be the same for most of the subsequent immigrants and settlers who have made Australia their home.

The culture of the Australian Aborigines, as well as the Torres Strait Islanders, was built up over the 60,000 to 65,000 years they have inhabited the vast country. The cultures of these indigenous populations are diverse and complex and have evolved over time, adapting and changing as needed. The traditions, religions, knowledge, and teaching were passed down through the generations, from one to the next, in the form of paintings and other art forms as well as with dance and rituals.

Historically, the original Australians were classified into the aforementioned two distinct groups of Aborigines and the Torres Strait Islanders. The former lived throughout the Australian mainland, while the latter inhabited the islands found between mainland Australia and Papua New Guinea in, as their name suggests, the Torres Strait. Some of the Indigenous cultures found in Australia are thought to be among the oldest in the world and compare with earlier cultures found in the caves in the southwestern areas of Palawan Island in The Philippines. These are the areas where, along with Indonesia, Australian Aboriginals most likely originated from.

At least 600 different Aboriginal "nations" were spread all around Australia. When the Europeans first arrived, each nation had its own language, laws, and tribal systems. The natives also lived in an assortment of different climatic conditions from the dry desert areas to the lush rainforests of North Queensland, and the colder areas of southern Australia and Tasmania.

Because of the different living conditions and areas they lived in, the different nations, tribes, or clans, all learned differing skills and developed their own unique lifestyles. For instance, these environmental differences were greatly reflected in the kind of shelter or clothing that particular tribes used. The specific needs of different tribes were shaped by weather and terrain but also by the animals that were found in the habitat, particularly dangerous ones.

Where conditions allowed, the highly mobile and nomadic Aborigines would use little more than a hollowed-out tree trunk for temporary shelter. Elsewhere, the shelters were much more complex, including huts, sleeping platforms, tents, and much more. Some of the Aboriginal clans are also known to have constructed windbreakers to protect themselves from the elements but also to make it easier to build and maintain fires. While many of the natives didn't use clothes almost at all, certain environments did necessitate the wearing of furs and other clothing items that protected the people.

Varying living conditions, of course, also drastically impacted the tools that were invented by individual clans. Hatchets, knives, spears, clubs, and the famous boomerangs were all constructed as needed, depending on the environment and the type of game that the Aborigines were after. Apart from living conditions and inventions, the habitat also dictated many traditions, ideas, and customs, giving rise to stark, fundamental differences between the many tribes.

Skirmishes occurred between the different groups, and they were known to practice cannibalism at different times. During the gold rush days, the settlers widely believed many Aboriginals liked to eat Chinamen because of their mainly clean diets and habits. They called them "long yellow pigs" and legend has it that they tasted sweet, while the Europeans tasted bad. There were many thousands of Chinese wandering the outback and gold fields looking for gold, unarmed and easy to capture. Once the gold hunters were caught, the tribes would use the traditional ponytails most of the Chinese wore to tie them in trees, so the victims could not escape until the cannibals wanted to eat them.

Just how many such stories were true remains a hotly debated topic, and the idea of Aboriginal cannibalism, in general, is a very controversial subject in Australia to this day. Historians who speak of historical, cannibalistic practices among the

Aborigines frequently come under fire from the indigenous people's descendants and opposing historians and anthropologists alike. While it has largely been established that cannibalism did occur, the point of most disagreement are the motives and the context for engaging in it.

Many experts explain that cannibalism occurred out of necessity and as a means of survival in dire conditions much more often than as a ritual. However, even when the indigenous folks did engage in cannibalism to avoid starvation, the practice would be approached in a very spiritual, ritualistic manner as a way of honoring the deceased or showing gratitude. This attitude may have facilitated the spread of the idea among the Europeans that the natives were engaging in cannibalism for the sake of religion and the cannibalistic act itself.

What's certain, however, is that the instances of cannibalism, whatever the underlying motive may have been, were naturally used by many of the early explorers and settlers to paint a certain unfavorable picture for the public. Therefore, it's easy to see why such stereotypes are an incredibly sensitive topic in Australia, especially when we consider the many instances of cannibalism among starving populations of virtually every civilization, even in the modern era, and particularly among shipwrecked crews and lost expeditions of Europeans themselves during the colonial times.

Apart from taking the stories of Aboriginal cannibalism with a grain of salt, it's also important to acknowledge other aspects of their lifestyle and culture, which paint a much different picture than the shallow notions of savagery and man-eating. The climatic conditions over most of Australia meant that it suited the nomadic lifestyle of the Aboriginals. They had a special relationship with the land, believing it was a living being. Every stick, rock, animal, and plant had a vital role, and they lived in harmony with their environment rather than trying to change it. They believed the land was the core of their spirituality, and they were one with the land.

Because of their unique relationship with the land and nature, the Aborigines were excellent hunters, and their knowledge allowed them to find water and track animals for food with ease.

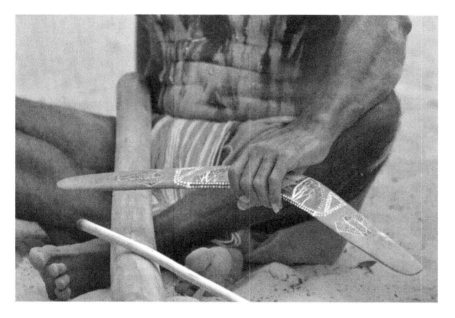

A series of national parks all around Australia contain and preserve some of the early rock art and cave drawings, which are an important part of the Aboriginal culture and heritage and their "Dreamtime." In the broadest sense, the term

"Dreamtime" is frequently invoked when one tries to give a name to the Aboriginal spirituality and their entire way of perceiving our world. A more accurate way of looking at it, however, is that Dreamtime is essentially the ancient time of creation, similar to Genesis for Christians.

The Aboriginals believe that their spirit ancestors created the world, then came and traveled the land in human form. As they traveled the land, they created the different plants and animals, as well as formed the Earth as we now know it. When they had finished the creation, they turned into the watering holes, streams and rivers, trees, and the stars in the sky. These areas have a special significance and spiritual properties as they are still, in essence, their spiritual ancestors who are alive and linking our past, present, and future together.

The Aborigines also believe that all of the tools that were necessary for their survival, such as hunting gear and weapons, were also bestowed upon them by the Spirits. They believe that Spirits gave the land and the habitat to individual tribes, as well as their totems and rituals. The bottom line is that Dreamtime refers to creation, as well as its continuation – the past, present, and future. As such, it represents the very foundation of

Aboriginal philosophy and faith, with all the smaller variations among the different cultures. As soon as one scratches the surface of this spiritual worldview, the importance of sacred Aboriginal sites becomes abundantly clear.

Australia is home to some very famous sacred sites; the best known one is Uluru, formerly Ayers Rock (its European Name). This site is in the center of Australia, about 250 km from the town of Alice Springs. Apart from the rock itself, caves in the rock are adorned with many sacred Aboriginal paintings. As is often the case, many of these paintings display various symbols and figures. The symbols often include concentric circles and other geometric objects. Being as old as they are, the meaning of much of these paintings is left to speculation, but common ideas behind concentric circles, for instance, are to mark a camping spot or a source of water. The figures represent outlines of various animals and their tracks. Some of the paintings, as a whole, were possibly created to tell a particular story, such as of a hunt in many cases, while also being used to teach the young.

Another sacred site in the area is known as Kings Canyon, a deep water filled canyon that also contains caves with many ancient cave paintings. But many of the important Aboriginal sites are kept from public knowledge as part of the Aboriginal law, both for the protection of the ancient sites from damage as well as by request of the Aborigines, as the local authorities and the natives, and have been given the rights to the land, jointly manage many of these sites.

The Aboriginal people did not have a written language, but recorded their folklore with dances and ceremonies as well as in their drawings and artwork. Part of everyday life was to learn the elaborate dances that were a unique part of their ceremonies. This would ensure that the traditions and stories of the various tribes would be preserved and passed down through the generations.

The visual arts have always been a very important part of Aboriginal culture. Today's rendering of the traditional and modern arts reflects the group awareness or spiritual understanding of many of the Aboriginal artists.

The indigenous visual art forms of today are no longer limited to paintings, but range from the remarkable dot paintings created in the central and western deserts in the 1970s to sculptures in wood, clay, ceramics, fiberglass, and the use of textiles. The Australian Cultural Council suggests that over a quarter of the aboriginal workforce is involved in the production or creation of some form of creative arts. Many widely accepted artists in both modern and contemporary dance and music perform in many parts of Australia.

Aboriginal tourism is also quickly gaining popularity and with a wide range of options, both for day trips and extended tours of many national parks and sacred Aboriginal sites. Now available in many areas of Australia, such tours give people a great insight into not only the modern lives of the Aboriginal people, but a better understanding of how they lived before the Europeans arrived.

The Origins of Aborigines

Like the rest of the *Homo sapiens,* the Aborigines descended from ancestors who migrated out of Africa in search of new lands to call their home. The aforementioned estimate of around 60,000 years ago is the most widely accepted theory as to how long ago the Aborigines made their way to Australia, but it's worth mentioning that some research has put their arrival even further back to over 100,000 years ago. Notably, the modern human departed Africa between 50,000 and 72,000 years ago. Therefore, the ancestors of the Australian Aborigines were most likely the very first wave to leave the continent.

Of course, the exact time when the migration began and when it started to split into different groups is still a point of quite a bit of contention, but the arrival of Aborigines in Australia seems to constantly coincide with the earliest movements of the modern human out of Africa. There also appears to be something of a trend in that the more genetic testing and other research that is done on Aborigines the further back their first arrival in Australia is pushed.

While the Aborigines are traced back to Africa, they certainly didn't come to Australia directly, much less across the Indian Ocean. In fact, their last stop before arriving in Australia was Southeast Asia or, more precisely, the current countries of Indonesia, Philippines, Singapore, Malaysia, and other places in the vicinity, where they arrived through the Southern Route. Many scholars believe these migrating people were indeed capable of constructing and successfully utilizing small and primitive boats to traverse certain waters. However, most of their journey was made on land, thanks to the fact that this was a time of lower sea levels, which meant that many land bridges that no longer exist were still there to facilitate human movement. In that regard, the migration of the Aboriginals to Australia was somewhat similar to how the Native Americans made their way to North America from Asia via the Bering Strait, which used to be a land bridge now called Beringia.

Research into the genetics of the Aboriginal people has also revealed a plethora of interesting findings. For one, an extensive research effort was made and published back in 2016 in *Nature,* the international journal of science, which conducted extensive studies into the DNA of indigenous Australians to find new, solid evidence that the ancestors of the indigenous Australians were indeed the first group to split from the waves of people migrating out of Africa.

While the researchers were confident that the question of how old the Aboriginal Australians are was now sealed, their study raised some other questions that weren't considered before. Namely, some of the modern indigenous Australians' genomes contain evidence that their ancient ancestors interbred with an unidentified branch of humanity. This human species was, by all indications, as separate as the Neanderthals or Denisovans.

The latter was a human lineage that originated from the Altai Mountains in Siberia, and this mystery species was seemingly related to them. This relation appears to have led previous researchers on to mistakenly identify this small part of the Aboriginal genetic material as Denisovan, which is turning out to be less than certain now. Whatever the truth may be, we will possibly get to know quite a few new things about the Aborigines in the coming years and decades, since these recent findings are bound to set more research efforts in motion. A few Aborigines with blond hair or blue eyes have been encountered over the years. Such phenomena have brought about many other theories as to who the Aboriginal Australians might have bred with over the centuries. Some have postulated that this is the result of fraternization and interbreeding between the natives and the colonists, but some other, extreme theories have really pushed the envelope. One example is the theory of Viking visitation to Australia hundreds of years before the first Dutch and British explorers. While the former proposition is possible and is being researched, the latter suggestion is largely unsubstantiated.

Defining the Aboriginal Australian

Historically speaking, the very term "Aboriginal Australian" defies definition as a particular people in the traditional sense. Nowadays, the term mainly defines a relatively small group of Australians (close to 700,000 people) whose indigenous ancestry is the main thing they have in common. In the colonial past, of course, an Aborigine was simply a native, but it's hardly correct or even fair to think of the Aboriginals, then or now, as a single, cohesive nation or a people. Doing so would mean denying the vibrancy and diversity of this ancient population. Hundreds of clans or rudimentary nations dotted the Australian landscape, and the differences between many of them were too stark to consider all of them a single group.

As mentioned earlier, the earliest classification of the natives was simply that of Aborigines and Torres Strait Islanders. As time went by and more was learned about these tribes, however, many of them were defined, studied, and named. In order to understand the complexity and diversity of Australia's indigenous population, the Aboriginals would undoubtedly need their own book, as the number of different clans and the cultures they created is incredible. Much has changed since the first European arrivals, though, and with the possible exception of some of the most remote areas in Australia, the number of Aboriginal folks whose ancestry is wholly indigenous has severely decreased. Nonetheless, the part of the population that can find indigenous ancestors in their lineage in one way or another is on the rise, and the population classed as indigenous is generally increasing.

Chapter 2: Early Explorers

An enduring misconception among many people is that the British were the first Europeans to set foot in Australia and explore the continent. In fact, the British played almost no part in the early explorations for quite a while until they started exploring and colonizing Australia in the 18th century. According to the vast majority of historians, the story of European exploration and contact with Australia begins in 1606, thanks to the Dutch.

The early explorers made no real attempts for quite a while to actually settle the new land, probably due to a lack of interest and awareness. The discovery of Australia was thus off to a rather slow start until a few arising factors sparked new interest and a need for further exploration and, ultimately, settlement. For 150 years, between 1606 and 1756, the Dutch were the dominant exploratory force in the uncharted southern lands, including Australia. This ambitious colonial force undertook some eight major expeditions in that time, sending nineteen vessels to Australia.

Also worth mentioning is the theory of Portuguese discovery, which has seen mixed reactions. Those who espouse the theory have evoked the old maps that Portuguese explorers charted on their voyages around the world for centuries. Namely, some of these maps do show a chunk of land southeast of India and Indonesia, but whether this land was charted through actual exploration is heavily contested, as rumors of an undiscovered southern land were going around among traders and explorers for centuries. As such, the "Australia" shown on these maps could have easily been a speculative addition. The Dutch first-hand contact and experience with Australia, on the other hand, is undisputed.

The Early Endeavors and the Arrival of the Dutch

Early in the fifteenth century, many European countries were exploring the world looking for new lands and riches such as gold and other precious metals. The Dutch were some of the most adventurous and aggressive of the early explorers; they believed there were many areas in the southern hemisphere where gold could easily be found.

The first of the Dutch sailors in these southern waters, Willem Janszoon, discovered Cape York in 1606 in what is now known as Queensland, Australia. When he and his crew landed, they thought the place was very inhospitable with its snakes, large crocodiles, sharks, and stinging jellyfish. The natives they encountered were also not very friendly, so he did not stay long. Willem Janszoon was also the first European to document his contact with the local Aboriginal people as he sailed and charted the east coast in his ship *The Duyfken*, which translates as "Little Dove."

Willem Janszoon's early life is largely a mystery, and his date of birth is only estimated to have been around 1570. Jansz, for short, as many called him, was a navigator in the service of the United East-Indies Company (VOC), and he spent quite a few years of his career serving in the Dutch East Indies, which mostly encompasses present-day Indonesia. Like most other navigators, sailors, captains, and other servants in the VOC fleet, Willem's duties generally included furthering the company interest and discovering new sources of trade and resources.

During that decisive year of 1606, Janszoon had already been on a three-year-long mission for the company, in charge of the

Duyfken since 1603. His trade-seeking assignment took him around the Dutch East Indies, where he visited various islands and fulfilled smaller exploratory tasks. In 1606, a rumor of gold reserves in New Guinea was going around, and Willem Jansz was tasked with investigating the information, which was the journey that took him from Jakarta to Australia.

The *Duyfken*'s voyage took Jansz and his crew to Cape York, Australia, after they made a southward turn through the Gulf of Carpentaria and reached the mouth of the Pennefather River, where they first discovered the coast of the new continent. Going back along the coast of the Cape York Peninsula, Jansz charted between 200 and 300 kilometers of the Australian coast and visited the Prince of Wales Island before approaching the coast of New Guinea again. Technically, Willem Jansz also found himself in the Torres Strait at one point, just weeks before Luis Vaez de Torres himself passed through it.

Torres was a Spanish explorer who was part of an expedition that was the first to successfully navigate through the entire Torres Strait, which separates Australia's Cape York from New Guinea. This expedition departed from Peru in December of 1605 with the belief in the existence of an unexplored southern continent waiting to be found. After a string of mutinous incidents and disagreements, the expedition's commanding officer, Pedro Fernandez de Quiros, got separated from the main group, effectively leaving Torres in command of two ships. Determined to fulfill his task, Torres sailed on until he reached the southern coast of New Guinea, later making his way to the strait that now bears his name. After navigating these treacherous parts and making contact with a few natives along the way, Torres finally made his way to the Philippines. Torres ended up essentially continuing right where the Dutchman Jansz left off just weeks before. *Duyfken*'s voyage would have probably gone on longer, and the ship could have been the first through the strait had the crew not started running low on supplies. They were also met with hostile action from some of the natives, which resulted in nine crewmen being murdered, although these clashes may have occurred in New Guinea. The indigenous folk were described later as "wild, cruel, black, and savage," in addition to being "man-eaters." Jansz had no earthly clue that he was, in fact, charting the coast of a new continent. He returned none the wiser, believing that the Australian peninsula of Cape York was connected to New Guinea. This simple oversight affected the accuracy of many a Dutch map for years thereafter.

In 1622, a less-known Dutch explorer by the name of Jan Carstenszoon was tasked with continuing Willem's earlier voyage and investigating the area further. Departing Ambon Island in January of 1623, Carstensz led the expedition consisting of two ships, *Pera* and *Arnhem*, toward New Guinea at first. Upon landfall in New Guinea, numerous members of the expedition were killed in an attack by the local natives. Shortly thereafter, the explorers headed further south until they spotted the Cape York Peninsula, close to present-day Port Musgrave.

Carstensz made contact with numerous Aboriginal folk in different parts of Cape York, and he noted that the natives living in the south were much friendlier than those who were further north, closer to New Guinea. Of the northern inhabitants, he said that many of them appeared to be familiar with European weaponry and capabilities. This was reflected in their retreat after warning shots would be fired from the crew's muskets, and also in their subsequent attempts to attack and ambush his men through adapted, yet seemingly guerrilla tactics.

The tribes in the southern parts of the peninsula were more docile, which allowed Carstensz and his men to interact and further examine their ways and culture. Many of them seemingly had no comprehension of firearms and other equipment fielded by the explorers. The natives calmly approached the visitors on numerous occasions and tried to take some of their items, which is believed to have been a custom of gift sharing as a sign of cooperation and concord between groups.

However, as some sources have later suggested, one of Carstenszoon's mission objectives was to "acquire" or, rather, kidnap at least one of the natives as a potential source of information. He and his superiors hoped that the indigenous folks could be interrogated as to the location of any valuable resources in the land. The Aboriginals were placated with gifts in order to earn their trust before the kidnapping, and there could have been at least a couple such incidents, sometimes resulting in deaths of the captives. Encounters like this also resulted in further conflicts and skirmishes where the expedition usually repelled attacks without much hardship. In general, Jan's report upon return to the Dutch East Indies was accurate and competent but unsatisfactory in regard to what he found, which contributed to a gradual loss of interest in the newly discovered lands.

During the years and decades that followed, other Dutch ships were sailing the Australian waters. These explorers also reported that most of the west and northern areas were barren and lacked water, making them of little economic value to the Dutch. They named the country New Holland, and it was also known as "Terra Australis Incognita," which translates to Unknown Southern Land.

Estimates show at least 54 European ships from a number of different countries visited Australia between 1606 and 1770. One of these ships, captained by Abel Tasman, was, like many others, sailing the southern hemisphere at that time, owned by the Dutch East-Indies Company. Abel Tasman charted much of the coastline of Australia and, later, had several areas named after him including the Tasman Sea and Tasmania.

Tasman's voyage started in 1642 when he was employed by Anthony Van Diemen, who was the Governor-General of the Dutch East Indies at the time. Tasman's assignment was to lead a far-reaching expedition into the largely uncharted southern waters. In August of that year, the expedition set sail from Batavia toward Mauritius, reaching the west coast of Tasmania in November. In honor of his superior, he named the location Van Diemen's Land, and the land was officially claimed shortly thereafter. In order to make this claim, Tasman's plan was to land at Tasmania's Forestier Peninsula, but the dodgy seas made this feat impossible. In spite of the stormy conditions, the ship's carpenter swam ashore and planted the flag.

Tasman's next order of business was to head north, but as fate would have it, unfavorable winds made him change his course eastward. Rough and dangerous seas were ahead, and the voyage was becoming increasingly difficult for the expedition, but through skilled seamanship and probably a bit of luck, Abel Tasman reached New Zealand. Abel and his men were thus also the first Europeans to reach this particular island. During their return, Tasman's crew was also the first to make a sighting of the Fiji Islands.

On his second voyage, which took place two years later, Tasman charted a good chunk of the northern Australian coast, starting at the northern tip of the Cape York Peninsula right under New Guinea and going all the way to North West Cape on the western coast of the continent. Tasman was also the man who named these newly charted lands "Nova Hollandia," or New Holland.

Despite the best efforts of Tasman and many brave seamen like him, nothing of value was ever found, which made these explorations seem like an increasingly ill-advised investment for VOC. Tasmania and New Zealand were completely neglected by Europeans for over a hundred years that followed, and mainland Australia itself didn't receive any major attention either.

The British Takeover

Things started to take a whole new turn toward the latter half of the 18th century when the British started getting more involved in the waters around Australia. An enduring belief that there was much more to be explored and quite possibly exploited played a big part in the revival of interest in the southern lands. On top of that, old imperial rivalries with France, the Netherlands, and Spain also further motivated the British to move in. As history now testifies, many rocks were indeed still unturned and the

British ever-lasting contribution to shaping Australia into what it is today had begun.

Captain James Cook, an Englishman, in his sailing ship *Endeavor* mapped the east coast of Australia and then on the 22 of August 1770, he claimed the east coast of Australia for the English King, George III and named it New South Wales. Captain Cook then sailed southeast and charted New Zealand and many of the islands of the South Pacific.

Captain Cook, who is now possibly the most famous of Australia's explorers, was an excellent navigator, but he was also an astronomer. As such, in 1768, he was formally sent on a mission to observe and document the transit of Venus over the Sun from a location in the South Pacific. Nonetheless, another one of his mission parameters was to search for new, vast land for exploration and potential exploitation, which was referred to as the "Great South Land." The location that his expedition headed to was Tahiti.

Cook was further instructed to explore the seas south of Tahiti after the planetary observation was complete. Furthermore, his next turn was to be westward, where he was to chart New

Zealand in detail and determine its true size. Lastly and perhaps most importantly in a historical sense, James Cook was told to proceed to Australia and chart its east coast, which was largely unexplored at that point.

Cook carried out his orders very successfully and, in 1770, he departed from New Zealand toward Australia. After sailing for a mere few weeks, Australia's southeast coast was in his sights. Captain Cook's expedition moved into what is now Botany Bay, as named by him, where the present-day city of Sydney lies. Shortly thereafter, the explorers proceeded north along the coast. Cook was detailed and meticulous in his mapping of the coast with all its bays, rivers, and other landmarks. HM *Endeavor* finally arrived at Possession Island in the Torres Strait in late August of 1770, where he formally declared that the east coast was now claimed for the King and named New South Wales.

This and James Cook's other subsequent voyages yielded much more information than just maps. For instance, he spent over 300 days in New Zealand, where he and his crew explored the flora and fauna as well. They wrote detailed, valuable scientific reports about their observations in nature, but Cook also provided a lot of information about the native Maori people –

information that holds up as useful to this day. He definitively proved that there was no major landmass between South America and New Zealand, which was believed by quite a few people at the time.

James Cook was also recorded as being an inquisitive, curious, and patient man who strove to understand the world around him. This kind of restraint made many of his encounters with indigenous people amiable and peaceful, especially by the standards of his time. Cook's career of exploration reached far and wide, so there were occasional skirmishes, of course, but he is generally remembered as a tolerant man, even when he was faced with true savagery such as cannibalism. James Cook's career ended at the age of 50 when he was killed by natives in Hawaii after a skirmish.

Other explorers, such as the English mariners George Bass and Matthew Flinders, made detailed maps of the Australian coast with the help of the French mariner Nicolas Baudin. They discovered that Tasmania was a separate island. This was largely uncertain in the time after Abel Tasman's discovery of the land and was now to be determined by the British. George Bass set sail in 1797 with instructions to proceed down the coastline south of Sydney, effectively picking up where Cook left off. He added some 300 miles of coastline to the maps, and he circumnavigated Tasmania and observed the currents around it, proving beyond any doubt that this was an island just south of Australian mainland. Flinders, on the other hand, undertook his charting journey in 1801 under orders to map out the remaining coastline. By 1803, his work was done and Australia was determined to be a single, vast island, with a solid idea of its entire coast now available to explorers.

Many areas have been named after the multitude of explorers who came to Australia during this time period. Some well-known examples of this are; Arnhem Land, Torres Strait, Tasmania, Dampier Sound, the Furneaux Islands, La Perouse, and Cape Freycinet. Apart from the explorers and their feats already mentioned, the other prominent seamen whose names these locations carry were William Dampier, Tobias Furneaux, Jean Francois de La Perouse, and Louis de Freycinet.

Chapter 3: First Settlers

The endeavors and discoveries made by James Cook and many other explorers sparked a lot of interest for the new southern landmass, and it seemed that this interest was increasing exponentially toward the late 18th century in Britain. The second half of the 18th century was quite an eventful time for Britain itself, but it was also a time of turmoil.

Britain and its allies emerged victorious from the Seven Years' War in 1763, which further motivated and bolstered the British imperial ambitions against their long-time rivals in Europe. However, the country was also going through a significant population increase, which, along with other factors, contributed to an increase in poverty. Of course, this kind of social instability carried with it an overall increase in crime and many of Britain's prisons were thus operating way over capacity. To make matters worse, the British also lost their 13 Colonies in the American Revolutionary War, so this land was no longer available. They needed somewhere else to send their convicts.

The Beginning – New South Wales

One of Captain James Cook's companions on his *Endeavor* voyage, a botanist by the name of Joseph Banks, was a distinguished supporter of establishing a British settlement and convict colony in Botany Bay. To that end, Banks suggested the idea to the crown in 1779, and his recommendation met an affirmative response. The British made preparations in the years that followed and the task was formally bestowed upon Arthur Phillip of the Royal Navy in 1786. Phillip's expedition set sail from England on May 13 of 1787.

They came in 11 ships commanded by Captain Arthur Phillip that held a total of 800-850 people including the crew and passengers, with some records putting that number as high as 1,400. This relatively small fleet, also known as the First Fleet, consisted of nine transport vessels, six of which were carrying convicts, as well as two warships for protection. The lead ship, captained by Arthur Phillip himself was called HMS *Sirius*. Apart from the fleet's crews, the passengers included over 700 convicts, who were mostly petty thieves from the poor parts of London either serving a sentence or recently convicted of such or similar crimes.

Although Arthur requested that his party consist of suitable candidates such as farmers, builders, and other skilled folks, his proposal was denied. Fourteen of the convicts' children were also onboard, which was a number that somewhat increased by the time the fleet reached its destination as the trip took eight months. Other personnel were comprised of marines on security details as well as a number of officers on each ship.

Captain Arthur Phillip was appointed Governor-designate by the British Home Secretary, Lord Sydney, and had instructions to build the first British Colony in New South Wales. He found that they were totally unprepared and had neither the equipment nor food supplies needed. They landed at Botany Bay between the 18th and 20th of January 1788 and found the area was not suitable for building their settlement. The seeds and plants they had brought with them did not suit the climate, and so they relocated to Sydney Cove in Port Jackson, better known as Sydney Harbor, on 26th January 1788. The colony had a difficult time because of the climatic conditions they encountered and the lack of provisions and basic food stocks. Social problems occurred in the colonies because there were four times as many men as women.

In addition to the shortages of supplies, the settlers experienced many other problems during the early stage. Establishing rule of law and overall stability in the colony was also no small task, and Arthur Phillip was burdened with the monumental responsibility of applying British law in a completely foreign land and upon a population that consisted mostly of convicts. To make matters worse, many of his officers were difficult to work with, as they all wanted benefits such as land, but a good portion of them was unwilling to put in the sweat and work for it.

Overall, the colony experienced significant hardships in sustaining itself. Finally, Phillip had no choice but to send one of his ships on a supply run all the way to Indonesia. Prior to that, a ship with supplies that was sent from South Africa to the colonys was wrecked along the way, which was why Arthur had no choice but to send out one of his own ships, HMS *Supply*. On top of that, the colony had already lost Arthur's own ship, HMS *Sirius*, on Norfolk Island, northwest of New Zealand.

The second fleet started arriving in Port Jackson in 1790, although the hopeful colonists were expecting HMS *Supply*'s return. This fleet was supposed to bring new settlers and convict labor for the colony, but it was known as the "Death Fleet" because the living conditions during the trip were so bad that 278 of the crew and convicts died on the voyage. This five-ship fleet was tasked with bringing in another group of over 700 convicts, but, this time, the fleet was operated by a private contractor. The nature of the business was such that it was most likely the reason behind such disregard for the convicts. Namely, the first ship to arrive was also the one that carried most of the fleet's supplies, which were necessary to feed the convicts along the way. Because of this, the settlers were denied basic necessities and, according to some records, this was done on purpose by the ship's commanders, who hoped to sell these essential supplies later. To make matters even worse, the shipmasters were the ones who would keep the allowance of each convict if he happened to perish along the way, which essentially incentivized neglect.

Apart from the fact that almost three hundred souls were lost, the remaining convicts themselves were in very bad shape, suffering from malnutrition, fevers, and various diseases. Instead of bolstering the colony's chances of prosperity and consolidation, these folks were thus an additional burden on the already-struggling settlers, making the situation even bleaker.

Nonetheless, HMS *Supply* successfully carried out her task, and a supply line was maintained with Norfolk Island. Apart from the numerous trips that this ship made in the time that followed, other vessels also began ferrying in help. After a rough start, the colony was starting to gradually stabilize in 1790, growing to around 2,000 people who were increasingly self-sufficient thanks to improving housing conditions and food production. By 1792, things were really starting to look optimistic, though Arthur Philip himself had fallen on harsh times due to his deteriorating health. Toward the end of the year, the Governor left New South Wales and headed back to England, leaving the colony under the authority of his military Lieutenant-Governors.

Consolidation and Relations with the Natives

Generally, when the first European explorers arrived in Australia and met with the native or Aboriginal people they found them to be friendly and easy to get on with. Once they managed to communicate and started trading, they found the Aboriginals were very interested in some western items like axes, knives, and shiny trinkets. The Aboriginal people also liked blankets, but were not very interested in clothes, as they did not wear them.

The early settlers essentially made friends with the local Aboriginal people, started trading with them for basic food and then developed farms in the Parramatta region about 25 kilometers inland on more suitable land. Governor Phillip was very active in gaining the help of the Aboriginal people for farming, hunting, fishing, and trading. At first, they were very cooperative, but when they discovered the settlers were taking their land and excluding them, they became understandably hostile.

Nonetheless, the first Governor continued to strive toward a good relationship with the indigenous folk. In fact, Arthur Phillip is remembered as one of the friendliest colonists of his time as he made every effort to be on good terms with the natives and make the British arrival mutually beneficial. He also made a friend of a local Eora native called Bennelong, and he even took this man back to England sometime later. Phillip's efforts to portray the colonists as trustworthy went so far that he was even wounded in a minor clash with a local tribe on one occasion after a misunderstanding, which was an attack he let go unanswered. He specifically instructed his men not to retaliate so as to avoid a cycle of violence.

As the colony was now stabilizing, New South Wales began to receive its first free settlers too. The first to arrive were but a couple of families in 1793, but the number of new arrivals began to grow steadily, and children were now being born regularly in the colony. All of this meant that some kind of conflict would likely be inevitable at some point, despite best efforts to avoid escalation. And besides, Arthur Philip had already left NSW at the time when the colony really started growing. The growing competition over land worked in unison with prejudice and a lack of understanding that many colonists had toward the natives to fuel more and more conflict as time went by. And, of course, this meant that some very dark times were ahead for the Aborigines.

The Aboriginals were either killed during confrontations with the settlers or driven away from the areas being farmed and settled. In the Sydney area, between 1790 and 1810, the Eora people and their leader, Pemulwuy of the Bidjigal clan, planned and undertook a series of attacks designed to frighten off the settlers. The Governor responded by placing a bounty on any Aboriginal, dead or alive, found in the areas where the colonies were located. The colonial and subsequent authorities also gave out licenses to shoot Aboriginals on sight, which caused any remaining Aboriginals to flee the area. The last of these licenses was revoked in 1957.

The Aboriginal attacks didn't always focus on the settlers directly. In fact, the natives were also known to attack specifically for the purpose of causing economic damage and making life difficult for the colony. To that end, the natives attacked sheep herds, horses, and cattle. They would also set crops and structures ablaze when they could. Significant attacks and clashes continued to occur well into the second half of the 19th century, and the Aborigines managed to drastically hinder the expansion of some colonies at times. The conflict raged throughout Australian lands, including Tasmania and other islands. The colonies were far from unwilling to reciprocate, though, and many massacres occurred through those decades, with perpetrators rarely suffering any legal repercussions.

A particularly famous incident occurred at Myall Creek, central New South Wales, in 1838. This was an unfortunate event where around thirty unarmed Aboriginal people were massacred by Europeans. Like most other similar atrocities, the Myall Creek Massacre saw a trial that essentially constituted a mere formality where the perpetrators were quickly acquitted. However, things took a novel turn when a second trial was held soon thereafter, finding many people guilty and even resulting in a few hangings. This highly documented case rippled through the colonies, caused a lot of controversy, and had a significant impact on relations between the Europeans and Aborigines.

Apart from violent confrontations, European settlements had a profound, devastating impact on the indigenous population in other ways. Like in many other instances of colonization elsewhere in the world, the white man brought over many diseases that decimated the locals in the subsequent years. The most notable of these afflictions, of course, was smallpox, which some experts believe may have exterminated as much as 50% of the Aborigines in the colonized areas. For instance, the smallpox outbreak began around 1789 in Sydney Cove, and, by 1791, the entire Cadigal Aboriginal clan was brought down to three surviving members.

Concerned that their colonial rivals might try to set up their own colonies elsewhere in the vast new continent, the British set out to settle the western parts of the continent, including the southern coast. The area of Albany was claimed in 1791 by George Vancouver, creating a new British colony in Western Australia for King George III.

New Holland, as Western Australia was still known at the time, had been in French sights for some time, which is why the British initiative was so decisive. Had the British not made their move on time, the history of Western Australia and the continent as a whole could have been much different. As fate would have it, the British claim was successful and just in time too, as there were numerous French expeditions in the area at that time and after the British annexation. The most crucial expeditions, however, were undertaken by the British. Apart from Matthew Flinders and others, another famous voyage that visited Australia was that of Charles Darwin aboard HMS *Beagle* in the 1830s.

The Rum Rebellion and Beyond

The relations within the colony of New South Wales itself were not always ideal, with a lot of politics and power play involved. The more the colony grew the more potential there was for certain settlers to get wealthy, and this caused quite a bit of competition between some of the colonists, particularly those in administrative positions. There were folks with high ambitions who were ready to take over and create monopolies in many areas of the colony's businesses.

After the departure of Arthur Phillip from the colony in 1792, he was succeeded as Governor by John Hunter (1795-1800), Philip Gidley King (1800-1806), and William Bligh, who ran the colony from 1806 to 1808. Bligh's term was so short because it ended abruptly in what would later come to be known as the Rum Rebellion. This incident was the first and only time that a military coup d'état was staged in Australia.

The perpetrators of the coup were members of the New South Wales Corps, the name given to the military forces stationed in the colony since 1792. In the years that followed the initial consolidation of NSW, young men who were raised in the colony were beginning to join the Corps, which eventually made this a rather unique military force. Over time, quite a few high-ranking members of the NSW Corps became involved in various businesses, some of which were very lucrative. A particularly common field of interest for these officers was the trade of spirits and other liquor, which they soon monopolized, earning them the nickname of "Rum Corps."

Monopoly brought the Corps money, and money brought them increasing influence and power, which, in Bligh's eyes, the officers were using to further their own interests above all else. As such, the Rum Corps became a threat to order but also to small businesses and farmers, whom they sought to stamp out as much as possible.

Aiming to curtail the Corps' influence and prop up small-time settlers, Bligh took steps to reassert his legitimate authority as bestowed upon him by the Crown. After a while of tensions and turmoil, Lt. Colonel George Johnston of the NSW Corps and his men arrested William Bligh and some of his staunch supporters on January 26 of 1808. The Rum Corps thus assumed total control over the colony and, given the distance from Britain, managed to rule until 1810, when the British government sent Lachlan Macquarie to take over as Governor and restore order to NSW. Once he assumed the office, Macquarie swiftly relieved all Corps-appointed officials of their positions, reinstated Bligh's people, and disbanded the New South Wales Corps, sending many of them back to Britain.

Chapter 4: Early Government

The Rapid Expansion of New South Wales

Before the legal system and institutions could grow in New South Wales, the colony itself needed to expand. Governor Macquarie's term lasted all the way until 1821, and it was quite eventful and important for the further development of New South Wales. One crucial aspect of Macquarie's term as Governor was his focus on building and improving the colony's infrastructure. Macquarie allocated funds and labor to improving the streets and built better housing for his troops. The colony also soon acquired the name of Sydney or Sydney Town, as it was indeed starting to look like a town.

Macquarie then set his eyes westward toward the Blue Mountains, which posed a significant barrier against further inland exploration and colonization. The Governor's aim was to find a passage through the mountains and evaluate the land that lay beyond, and numerous explorers were given this task. Much of the colony's farming activity was thus far concentrated around Parramatta, just west of Sydney, but the prospect of new, arable land was of untold potential and importance at that time, especially considering the number of people arriving as fresh settlers.

Just three years into Macquarie's term, in 1813, explorers William Lawson, William Wentworth, and Gregory Blaxland managed what quite a few folks before them could not do. The trio of explorers, along with a handful of servants, dogs, and horses set out on this all-important endeavor in May of 1813. After crossing over sixty miles of rugged terrain and forests, they managed to chart a path beyond the mountains. What they found were rich, expansive plains of very suitable land that they estimated could feed the colony for decades. This discovery was of immense economic significance to New South Wales, and the town of Bathurst was quickly established west of the Blue Mountains. From that point on, the colonies finally began to rapidly expand inland, which also facilitated further exploration for decades thereafter.

With the acquisition and settlement of so much new, valuable land, another important impact for NSW was a growing need for more laws and regulations, particularly in regards to real estate. The first attempts to consolidate order saw the colonial authorities establish thirteen counties within a 200-mile radius around Sydney, prohibiting any use of the lands beyond that line. The radius was created toavoid potential chaos when individual explorers and other settlers working independently would decide to go beyond the frontier and claim anything in sight to be used as they saw fit.

Although a legitimate concern, the order was difficult to enforce. Many influential and ambitious businessmen routinely sent their servants, employees, and other laborers well beyond the frontier to use the land to feed their livestock at first. Soon enough, land was being outright claimed. The lack of control affected the stability of the colony, but the indigenous populations saw the brunt of the problem who saw their land taken and many of their kin forcibly removed through violence and murder. Despite these growing pains, roads were being built through the Blue Mountains, the colony was becoming more interconnected, and a legal system and effective governance were certainly on the horizon.

New South Wales remained a penal colony until 1823. Its population was made up of a small number of free settlers that came on the early ships, but mainly convicts, their guards and marines, as well as the wives of quite a few folks from all these groups. Once the convicts had served their prison time they were released and allowed to settle anywhere they chose. This is how the number of free settlers began to grow rapidly in addition to the expansion of the colony's area.

The system of emancipation and land acquisition for former convicts was in place the whole time, ever since Arthur Phillip first established the colony. Upon expiration of their sentence, ex-convicts were given a strong incentive to stay and build up the colony. As a baseline, some 30 acres would be given to recently emancipated convicts on the condition that they would put in the work to cultivate the land and do everything they can to make it prosperous. Perks such as the ability to acquire substantially more than 30 acres if a man wanted to marry and start a family stimulated growth. . The authorities provided everything that the settlers needed to work their land, from livestock to tools to food assistance. Vowing to stay for the long haul also meant that the land would come free of all taxes, with the condition that the settler would have to provide suitable wood for the Royal Navy, assuming that an individual estate produced such material. Given these extensive measures and subsidies, the NSW colony grew so quickly. Simultaneously, developing a strong and stable rule of law as soon as possible was crucial.

The Government and Land

In 1823, the British government established the first New South Wales Parliament, setting up a Legislative Council and then the Supreme Court. Under an act of The English Parliament in London, the act was known as the 1823 New South Wales Judicature Act (UK). The first step in creating a new Government in Australia, the act gave the free people and the convicts both criminal and civil courts to air their grievances.

Another important development occurred in 1829, when it was decided by the Crown that the people born in Australia, regardless of race or color, would become a British subject by birthright. This development was essentially the official British claim over all of Australia, brought on by the annexation and colonization of the Swan River Colony that same year. The French were now clearly denied their aspirations toward Australian lands, and the British annexation was solidified. The Swan River Settlement in Western Australia later acquired the name of Perth, which remains one of Australia's major urban centers and the capital of its state.

While things were going smoothly for the British, the Aborigines, on the other hand, were in for some very rough times from that point onward. The government did not recognize the indigenous land owners until the 1830s when there were two land treaties signed between John Batman and the Kulin Aboriginal people for 600,000 acres of land between Melbourne and the Bellarine Peninsula, though the attempt failed.

This attempt, for the first time, acknowledged that the Aboriginal people owned the land and had the "right" to sell it. Sir Richard Bourke, the NSW Governor, was not happy about this arrangement as it would set a precedent that others would follow. He issued a proclamation that stated that all the land of Australia belonged to no one before the British crown had taken possession of it and all land now belonged to the British Crown.

The British Colonial Office agreed with Governor Bourke and issued another Proclamation that stated, "Any person found in possession of any land they did not have the express permission of the government to occupy would be treated as trespassers." The crown owned all the land claimed by Captain Cook on 22 August 1770, under instructions from King George III of

England. Before this claim, the land was owner-less, even though the "House of Commons" had recognized in 1873 that Aboriginal occupants had the legal rights to their land. In order for anyone (anyone is singular, so use he instead of they) to claim a title to any land, he first had to purchase it from the government whether he was Aboriginal or from another country. The Australian courts used this ruling from 1830 until 1992 when the High Court recognized the traditional land ownership and rights of the Australian Aboriginal in the "Mabo" Lands Rights Case in 1992.

In 1861, The Crown Land Act permitted any person, regardless of his country of origin, to select and obtain a title to a section of Crown land of up to 320 acres to settle on the condition that a suitable deposit had been paid. He would also have had to occupy (live on) the land for at least three years. This Crown Land Act had the effect of limiting the Aboriginal people's right of access to these newly formed pastoral and farm lands. Up until this time, much of this land was the traditional home and hunting lands of the Aboriginals who lived in those areas.

This opening up of the land to new settlers resulted in many conflicts between the various groups who were competing for the land, including the new landowners, the Aboriginals who were living there, various squatters, and the government agents who were charged with selecting who could claim the land titles.

Huge areas of what was vacant land were now being claimed, which caused many disputes and resulted in a relatively large number of people becoming fugitives from the law. Some, because they missed out on getting a property, turned to a life of crime, such as the famous bushranger and highwayman Ned Kelly. Other people tried to use elaborate schemes to swindle others from their legally obtained property; they were known as bushwhackers.

Despite all the problems people faced, the former penal colony of New South Wales grew and prospered. The area where the first British Colony started, The Port Jackson Settlement, is now Sydney, which has become Australia's largest city. John Batman, the Founder of Melbourne

John Batman was, by all indications, a checkered man who remains a figure of significant controversy to this day. While his contribution to Australia's development and his legacy are immense, many people back then as well as today have raised quite a few grievances as to the man's character and conduct. John Batman is a polarizing figure in Australia's present discourse, folks commonly identify with particular political alignments based on their perception of this man.

John Batman was recorded as being a rancher, explorer, and entrepreneur. He was born in the Parramatta settlement of New South Wales in January of 1801 to parents who arrived in 1797, making him a native of Australia. His father was brought over to Australia as a small-time convict, but John's mom was able to pay for the fare and follow her husband with their son and daughter, ensuring that the family stayed together in the new continent. The couple had an additional four sons in Australia, including John, and the family mostly prospered in a stable, ordinary life, especially after John's father's sentence was served in 1810.

John left home in 1816 to become a blacksmith apprentice, before proceeding to learn all manner of different trades. Just five years later, in 1821, John and his brother Henry set out to Van Diemen's Land to seek their fortune, and they established themselves in the northeast of the island, near Ben Lomond, where they acquired a property sometime later. John also married an escaped convict by the name of Eliza Callaghan in 1828.

Batman started rising to prominence due to his intelligence and many talents, and he was recorded by those who knew him as being a man of logic, focus, and high motivation. He had sophisticated social skills, which frequently landed him in circles much above his own class. John also engaged in various forms of public service. Most notably, he pursued bushrangers and other outlaws and, quite famously, he was the man who brought the notorious, English-born robber Matthew Brady to justice in 1826.

The question is, however, how did John Batman come to be labeled by some as a murderer and criminal? One of Batman's neighbors at Ben Lomond, John Glover, called him a rogue, thief, liar, and a cheat. Above all, he referred to Batman as a murderer of blacks and the vilest man that Glover had ever known. George Augustus Robinson, the Chief Protector of Aborigines in Port Phillip, Melbourne from 1839 to 1849, was also very critical of the man, calling Batman a bad and dangerous character.

The main controversies of John Batman's life fell into the larger context of a particularly important historical event in Australia, which was the "Black War" in Tasmania, then Van Diemen's Land. This event was a conflict between the settlers and the Aborigines, which saw the greatest intensity between the mid-1820s and late 1830, ultimately leaving a few hundred settlers and at least one-thousand Aborigines dead. Toward the end of the conflict at that time, Batman was a part of the so-called "Black Line," which was essentially a military operation with the goal of routing the remaining Aborigines.

Prior to these events, during the 1820s, Batman also made his name by being quite assertive and taking a lot of initiative in going after the indigenous tribes. Toward the late 1820s, Batman sought approval from the Governor, which was granted, to form his own "Roving Party," which would fight along the frontier and push the Aborigines back. Many historians agree that the opportunistic John Batman used the larger conflict with the Aboriginal people to forward his own entrepreneurial interests. Several of his combat expeditions yielded lofty rewards in the form of valuable land. The colonial authorities also rewarded him with live prisoners.

Perhaps somewhat ironically, John Batman made history when, in 1835, he attempted to affect the so-called Port Phillip Association agreement with the Aborigines around present-day Melbourne. He famously failed at buying land from the Aborigines instead of just forcibly taking it, which is what made it such a unique case. The authorities cracked down on the deal, as the agreement would have certainly set a precedent.

Overall, John is widely remembered as a pioneer of Melbourne and one of its founders, and he was undoubtedly a successful businessman in his time. And interestingly he, a perceived opportunist, scoundrel, and killer was one of the incredibly rare few who tried to acquire land by peaceful means, even if it was merely a business decision. John Batman died in 1839 from syphilis and quite a few other health complications.

The Exploits of Edward "Ned" Kelly

As history has shown us very clearly, a government in its infancy with inadequate rule of law make fertile ground for crime on a level mostly unfathomable to modern sensibilities. In turn, this can give birth to some very (in) famous criminals that go on to become the stuff of legend for generations to come. One such individual was Ned Kelly, the famed bushranger, gang leader, and killer of police officers.

Born thirty miles north of Melbourne in Beveridge in 1855, Ned Kelly was the son of an Irish convict, John Kelly, also known as Red. After his father died at Ned's young age of eleven, he gave up on school and instead went to live and work with his grandfather who was a cattle farmer. From the very get-go, Ned was a problematic boy who often came into contact with the law. As such, just three years later, fourteen-year-old Ned was arrested for assault when he allegedly attacked a Chinese farmer. This crime landed young Ned in jail for a mere seven weeks, but his life of crime was only beginning. Only a year later, in 1870, Ned was charged with another assault in addition to theft of a horse, which was found in his possession at the time. This time, the authorities saw fit to incarcerate him for three years. The jail time most likely did little more than consolidate Ned's criminal mind and push him further away from any semblance of a socially acceptable way of life.

His life took a particularly decisive turn in 1878. Namely, after an altercation revolving around the honor of Ned's sister Kate, Ned fired his gun at a police constable by the name of Alexander Fitzpatrick, though he just injured the man's wrist instead of killing him. As the incident occurred at the Kelly residence, multiple members of Ned's family were involved, with his mother Ellen also being charged and sentenced with a crime. Ned's brother Dan and even a couple of neighbors were also implicated in the attack. However, all of this was mostly taken from Fitzpatrick's word when he went back to the police station. What exactly transpired can be debated, but, reportedly, Fitzpatrick was drunk and went to the Kelly residence to serve a dubious warrant, after which he started to harass Kate. This side of the story was mostly taken from a letter that Ned wrote sometime later, detailing the incident as well as other instances of police abuse against his family.

Whatever the truth may have been, this direct conflict with the local law enforcement was enough to push Ned over the edge.

And so, Ned and his brother Dan, along with two partners in crime Joe Byrne and Steve Hart, ran away to become outlaws and form the famed Kelly Gang. Not long after they went out into the Australian bush, they came into contact with a police posse that was sent out to apprehend them. The officers were ambushed, leaving three of them dead and earning the gang members a lofty bounty on their heads.

The gang then turned full-time to robbing banks in the more rural settlements in the countryside. They weren't leaving anything to chance, however, and so they used some of their stolen money to build their signature equipment – steel armor. The Kelly Gang met its demise shortly thereafter in 1880. This came during their ambitious plan to derail and rob a potentially valuable train that was expected to arrive at Glenrowan, Victoria, on June 29 from Melbourne. The gang's plan was to force two railway workers to destroy a portion of the tracks in order to stop the train, after which they were to storm out from the local hotel and commence the robbery. To that end, they captured a hotel in Glenrowan and took around sixty hostages.

An act of kindness cost them dearly, however, after a family whom Ned freed sent out a warning to the authorities. Not long after that, the police arrived instead of the train, surrounded the premises, and a dramatic shootout occurred. The gang was later found to have been significantly sleep-deprived and intoxicated, and their armor was much less effective than they anticipated. As such, the robbers didn't stand much of a chance and everyone except Ned Kelly was killed while he was wounded. The fearsome Ned himself was captured, tried, convicted, and hung by the neck until dead in 1880.

Chapter 5: The States and Territories of Australia

Australia's present-day structure includes two distinct entities of administrative division – states and territories. States enjoy a significant level of autonomy with their own constitutions, local governments and parliaments, which can decide on issues that are outside the jurisdiction of the Commonwealth according to Section 51 of the Australian Constitution. The six states are Queensland, New South Wales, South Australia, Tasmania, Victoria, and Western Australia.

Territories, on the other hand, are mostly separated by little more than administrative lines, with the exception of the Northern Territory and the Australian Capital Territory (ACT), which both have limited autonomy and are usually de facto seen as states. These two, along with the Jervis Bay Territory, are also the only territories connected to or located on the Australian mainland. However, Jervis Bay is governed only by Commonwealth law, albeit by an Australian administrator. Other such territories include many islands such as Ashmore and Cartier Islands, Christmas Islands, Coral Sea Islands, as well as Australia's territorial claims in Antarctica. All of these territories and states each have their own piece of the larger Australian story.

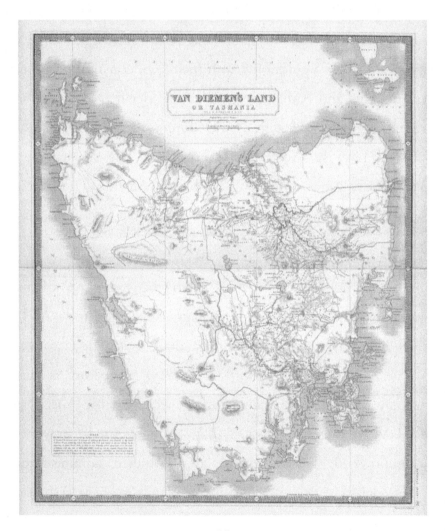

Van Diemen's Land

Tasmania, originally known as Van Diemen's Land, is by far the largest island in Australia and is today home to over 500,000 people. While Tasmania's European history, began in the mid-17th century, the island wasn't settled until well over a century later. Lieutenant John Bowen landed at Risdon Cove with a small group to establish the first British settlement on the island in 1803. The group was made up of former sailors, settlers, convicts, and soldiers, but this site was soon changed in favor of a new site.

The change was mainly a result of Bowen's request. A few months after he made landfall at Risdon Cove, Bowen went to Sydney officially to bring in a robbery suspect, but his main motive was to ask for a transfer and be relieved of his duties in the settlement, as he wanted to join the war against France. Governor King of NSW then instructed him to resettle to Derwent or Port Dalrymple and give the Risdon settlement over to David Collins.

Bowen was too slow in catching up to Collins, however, and David had already sailed for Derwent to move the settlement, after which he established a settlement at Sullivan's Cove, which later became Hobart, Tasmania's capital and largest city. The government officially changed the island's name to Tasmania in 1856 after the explorer Able Tasman.

Western Australia

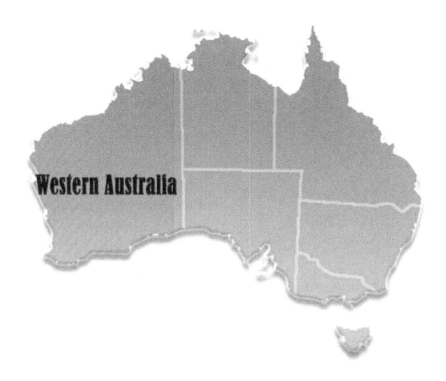

The first British settlement was built at King George's Sound (Albany), Western Australia, in 1827 by Major Edmund Lockyer. Two years later, the Swan River Colony (which later became Western Australia) had its first Governor, Captain James Stirling. In 1849, Western Australia became a British penal settlement with the first group of convicts arriving there in 1850. These early settlements around Albany played an integral and decisive role in the British claim over Western Australia and thus the entire continent, and that very first arrival at Albany in 1826 came three years before the Swan River Colony was officially claimed.

The Swan River Settlement was of particular importance, as it later became Perth, the capital of the state and one of the largest cities on the continent with around 1,800,000 residents. This important city has played a prominent role in Australia's growth and has been host to many important events, such as the Commonwealth Games of 1962. Albany is one of the fastest-growing cities in the country and among WA's largest at over 35,000 residents. Prior to being recognized as a state under the new Australian constitution, WA had already become self-governing in 1891.

South Australia

The British province of South Australia was first established in 1836 and became a crown colony in 1842. Two years before that, the city of Adelaide, now the capital, was founded through Australia's first democratic election. Although a large number of ex-convicts settled in South Australia, it was never used as a convict colony. By 1850, over 38,000 immigrants and ex-convicts were living there.

The 1850s were of great importance for many Australian future-states, especially South Australia, Tasmania, Victoria, and New South Wales. In 1850 and 1851, South Australia, along with Tasmania and Victoria, formed their first legislative councils through elections, after the British Parliament passed an act that granted them representative government. 1855 was another landmark year because South Australia, Tasmania, Victoria, and NSW were given the right of partial self-governance by Britain. In 1856, the Australian ballot was also introduced and combined with secret voting, which became a voting standard in much of the world. Toward the end of the century, in 1896, South Australia also gave voting rights to everyone over the age of 21, including women and indigenous people.

Victoria

Lieutenant David Collins made the first attempt at settling Victoria in 1803, but this effort was interrupted when he was given orders to resettle to Hobart Tasmania in 1804 instead. The Henty brothers, the first Europeans to establish meaningful agriculture in Victoria, landed in 1834 at Portland Bay to start a settlement that was eventually to become the City of Melbourne. When John Batman settled there, the Port Phillip District became officially sanctioned. Port Phillip's first immigrant ships arrived in 1839.

Victoria and the Port Phillip District officially separated from New South Wales in 1851. This was generally the result of petitions and other initiatives by the locals over a period of around ten years. A significant breakthrough came in 1850 when the colony of Victoria was officially established via the Australian Constitutions Act. After a few months, the newly established colony was given its legislative council. The separation was not a result of any serious hostility but was instead motivated by economic misgivings. The split also gave rise to an ongoing economic competition between the states and their respective capitals, Sydney and Melbourne, which has served to greatly invigorate progress and growth. Melbourne has since become a major urban center that is renowned all over the world, has repeatedly been ranked as the most livable city on the planet, and even hosted the Summer Olympic Games in 1956.

Queensland

Lieutenant John Oxley established the Moreton Bay Settlement penal colony at Redcliffe in 1824. The colony then moved to an area now known as Brisbane with about 2,280 convicts sent there between 1824 and 1839. In 1838, the first of the free European settlers moved to the district, soon to be followed by many others. Once the city of Brisbane was established, it split away from New South Wales to separate into an individual state called Queensland.

Queensland's democratic development was taking off rapidly in the 19th century. Only two decades after the free settlers started flocking in, Queensland introduced secret voting in 1859 and was granted self-governance. Six years later, all indigenous folk were given the right to participate in state elections. Brisbane, the capital of Queensland, grew exponentially and is now populated by over two million people. 1982 saw Brisbane as the host of that year's Commonwealth Games.

Northern Territory

The Northern Territory was originally, like most of Australia, part of the New South Wales penal colony. The first European settlers established themselves at Fort Dundas, Port Essington around 1824. South Australia took control of the area in 1863 and, in 1869, Palmerston Town was successfully settled. This settlement was later known as Darwin and became the capital of the Northern Territory. The Northern Territory became a part of the Commonwealth of Australia on 1st January 1911 when it separated from South Australia.

The conditions for the early settlers were so harsh due to the dry, hot environment that the colonial authorities imported thousands of camels to help with exploration, which is why some 200,000 wild camels now live in the Northern Territory. This land is also the location of the oldest river system in the world belonging to the Finke River. A large concentration of Aboriginal people live in the NT, amounting to around a quarter of the total 250,000 people that populate it. As such, this territory is a major center of the enduring Aboriginal culture and identity with over 80 different languages and many cultures still in existence. In addition to many sacred sites and national parks such as Kakadu, the Aborigines own around a half of the total land area of the Northern Territory.

New South Wales

Being the longtime economic, cultural, and political center of European expansion into Australia, New South Wales is still something of a core for the modern Australian State. Remaining the most populous state at close to eight million people, although the eternally competing Victoria isn't too far behind with over six-million.

In 1835, the Australian Patriotic Association was created by W. C. Wentworth to demand that New South Wales had the right to form a democratic government. In 1843, the legislative council held its first parliamentary election.

NSW's institutions began growing and so did its autonomy and stability, especially after the NSW Parliament was established in May of 1856. This landmark achievement propelled the colony into a bright future of exponential development. Two years later, male inhabitants over 21 years of age were granted the right to vote.

New South Wales is home to many cultural landmarks to this day, especially in the city of Sydney, which is the largest city in all of Australia. One famous example is the Sydney Opera House, which was opened in 1873. Due to this and other attractions, Sydney draws in a considerable amount of tourists and world attention, and it's also frequently a host of many important events such as the 2000 Summer Olympic Games.

Australian Capital Territory (ACT)

Unique in many regards, the Australian Capital Territory is located within New South Wales hosting the nation's capital, Canberra. ACT is the only landlocked unit in all of Australia encompassing the city and a piece of land that stretches somewhat to the southwest and then a longer way south toward the Scabby Range Nature Reserve. On its territory, ACT also includes the Bullen Range Nature Reserve and the Namadgi National Park. Overall, it is by far the smallest territory in Australia with only 2,358 square kilometers, which translates to less than 1% of Australia.

Before European settlement, the area around Canberra was home to the Ngunnawal Aborigines, who are believed to have lived there for some 21,000 years. In the vicinity, there were also the Gundungurra, Ngarigo, Wiradjuri, and Yuin peoples. The settlement began with Joshua John Moore, a British grazier and real-estate entrepreneur, who set up his station at Acton in 1823 and named it "Canberry." The town that grew out of Moore's property was chosen as the Australian capital in 1908, and the Australian Capital Territory was officially proclaimed in 1911. After further expansion and consolidation, the Australian Parliament was set up in the city in 1927.

Chapter 6: The Growth of Australia and the Gold Rush

A gold mine in Western Australia

Many of the first European, or white people, that immigrated to Australia had no choice as they were convicted and sent there from England as convicts, or they were the guards and soldiers sent to control the convicts. By 1820, many of the convicts won their freedom and received land to farm and to earn a living.

Many of these people turned their lands into flourishing farms. The news of this quickly spread around the world, and people knew that Australia had large amounts of very cheap or even free land as well as a large labor shortage. Anyone willing to work could quickly prosper and even become wealthy. The new world was the ideal place to raise a healthy, happy family. People from all around the world started arriving, by the boatload.

Soon, all the land around the main settlements was taken, so the newcomers started moving deeper into the interior and spreading around the coast line. This expansion meant they were moving deeper into Aboriginal territories, which could mean trouble, so they were usually heavily armed. Available land was becoming hard to find due to the growing number of settlers and farmers were becoming desperate to find good grazing areas with water in some colonies.

Then in the 1850s, gold was discovered, and the rush was on. A huge influx of people started converging on the goldfields of Victoria and NSW from all around the globe, including China, USA, Canada as well as all parts of Europe. The prospect of gold also lured thousands of people from around Australia and New Zealand. With the prospectors, (those that actually do the digging and gold-finding work) came a large assortment of those who live off the miners, including publicans, entertainers, prostitutes, illicit liquor sellers, gamblers, quacks, and all manner of thieves.

Although gold was officially discovered by Edward Hargraves near Bathurst in eastern New South Wales in 1851, numerous smaller discoveries were made in other places. The Blue Mountains, Tasmania, and many other locations were known by some to have at least small traces of gold as early as 1841. However, this information was kept on a need-to-know basis at that time because the authorities feared the reaction of the many convicts in the colonies to the sudden discovery of gold. The possibility of an all-out rebellion and total collapse of the colonies was taken as a legitimate concern.

Things took a turn in the late 1840s, however, as news of the gold rush in California began to reach Australia. This prospect led to something of an exodus in some settlements, as free settlers and emancipated convicts started to abandon Australia in the hopes of making their riches in America. Things got so bad in some parts of the Australian colonies that there was a shortage of labor, which significantly affected the economy.

This led the authorities to change their whole approach to gold, and Australia's reserves of the precious metal were unveiled to the world in 1851 on the decision of New South Wales Governor Charles Fitzroy. Fitzroy aimed to revitalize the economy of his colony through gold, and he decided to have the rumored locations investigated. To that end, the Governor proclaimed that any man who found a significant amount of gold was eligible for a lofty reward.

After his failed gold-rushing endeavor in California, Edward Hargraves decided to try his hand at this new opportunity, and he returned to New South Wales in 1851. He was a capable man involved in many trades and businesses, as well as a sailor. Edward formed a team of helpers in Bathurst and headed inland in January. Not long into the expedition, Edward and his companions detected gold at Ophir, northwest of Bathurst. He was back in Sydney as soon as March to show the Governor samples of what he had found. Fitzroy's British government-appointed geologist was tasked with investigating the site of discovery, which he deemed viable. Edward was given a 10,000-pound reward, and the news of gold went out quickly.

Soon enough, gold was being found in numerous places all over the colonies. The massive influx of people thereafter was a major turning point in Australian history which significantly contributed to the exponential growth of its settlements and colonies. In 1852 alone, close to 400,000 migrants stormed the continent, which created a population spike of truly epic proportions considering that, prior to 1851, there were about 77,000 European settlers in Australia. The transportation of convicts to Australia still continued, but ceased in 1868.

The discovery of gold in New South Wales had essentially the same effect on Victoria that California had on NSW. Not to be outdone and devoid of valuable laborers, the Victorian authorities offered their own reward to any men who found gold around Melbourne. The efforts were a major success, and gold was struck in Ballart, Castlemaine, Bendigo, and other places. What's more, the gold reserves were much greater than those in New South Wales, and Victoria quickly became a major gold producer on the global stage.

In Victoria, the authorities were finding it hard to keep order and control because of the large numbers of transient people. In order for the authorities to enforce the law, the British

Governor brought out a system of licenses and fees. Introduced both by Fitzroy in NSW and Charles La Trobe in Victoria, this system was envisioned as a means of curtailing the unbearable onslaught of migrants and allocating additional funds for the budget as the colonies were quickly becoming unsustainable. All miners were now to pay thirty shillings a month to acquire a mining license.

From the very get-go, this was quite a sum for the miners, many of whom were only aspiring gold producers with little to show for their efforts at the time. The fees were immediately met with disapproval, but as the population continued to grow and the gold production decreased, disapproval started to evolve into fury. The miners were organizing and gathering to protest, and the politically-savvy among them formed delegations to negotiate with Governor La Trobe, but most of their requests and arguments fell on deaf ears. Instead of meeting their demands halfway, the Governor dispatched the police to crack down on any unlicensed mining. Instead, the miners claimed the police mostly just tried to extort money from them and commit other abuses of power.

The protests and gatherings continued, and outbursts of violence started to occur as well. Things took a bloody turn in October of 1854 when a Scottish miner was murdered at the Eureka Hotel in Ballart after a physical conflict. The owner of the hotel was accused and put on trial, but the process was rushed, and the man was promptly released. This sparked outrage among the miners who firmly claimed that one of the court officials was corrupt and routinely bribed by the accused. Following a mass protest of the court's ruling, a group of protestors burned down the Eureka Hotel in retaliation.

The perpetrators were arrested, but the well-organized miners, who had become very political by this point, elected a delegation to negotiate the release of the prisoners with the new Governor, Charles Hotham. The Governor would not hear it, and he chose to deploy 150 troops as reinforcement to his existing troops and police officers. Things were escalating and rapidly approaching the breaking point.

After the sour meeting with the Governor, the miners convened once again at Bakery Hill, where they discussed further action and began flying their own Eureka flag. The following morning, the police decided to conduct another license inspection sweep,

103

which, unbeknownst to them, pushed the protestors over the edge. After the police concluded their operation, the miners headed back to Bakery Hill and chose Peter Lalor, an Irishman, as their leader. After returning to the Eureka diggings, the protestors ceremonially took an oath to stand by each other and fight for their rights and liberty.

The determined protestors proceeded to build a stockade and set up a defensive perimeter, anticipating armed conflict to erupt soon. Surely enough, combined police and military forces were sent to disperse the protestors and remove the stockade on December 3. In the ensuing skirmish, 21 men and one woman died among the miners along with six soldiers. Over a hundred rebels were arrested, and thirteen stood trial in Melbourne.

Although, as would be expected, the miners lost the battle, their efforts were not in vain as they won some substantial human rights issues and gained a lot of support. The people of Victoria strongly disapproved of how the Eureka Stockade was handled, and the jury ultimately released all thirteen of the miner leaders. In the administrative proceedings that followed, the mining fee was abolished and, in its place, an export duty was introduced along with a one-pound yearly payment called a miner's right.

The police forces in charge of the Eureka diggings area were lustrated heavily, with around half of them being fired. Victoria's legislative council was expanded with twelve new members, one of whom was Peter Lalor, the leader of the rebellion.

The government also passed a parliamentary bill granting the right to any digger who held a miner's license to vote and stand for election. This is usually viewed as the very beginning of the Australian democratic system in practice today. The incident even sparked a few social experiments later on, some of which have become a world standard, such as the eight-hour work day. The formation of the Australian Labor Party also drew its origins from these crucial historical events. While the rebelling miners lost in the shootout, their eventual legal victory was so immense that it affected the course of the entire country and much of the world.

Chapter 7: Becoming a Nation

Before 1900, Australia was divided into six colonies that were all subject to British law. The British Parliament voted to grant the six colonies permission to form their own government. The consent was conditional on the government being formed in accordance with the Australian constitution which was written by public representatives from each of these six colonies from information and instructions they collected from a series of conventions in the 1890s and accepted by a referendum that was conducted in each colony.

Australia's six colonies/states became a single nation under a single constitution on 1 January 1901, marking the official birth of the Commonwealth of Australia, with Edmund Burton being elected as the first Prime Minister.

Under the Australian Constitution, the head of Australia or Australian monarch is the reigning British monarch. They are the Australian head of state and the Constitution grants them governing powers, placing them above all the other levels of the government in Australia. As Australia is so far from Britain, the monarch is able to appoint a Governor-General who can exercise in their absence the monarch's powers as needed.

The Australian Federal System

The Australian Constitution created what is known as a 'federal' system of government. Under this federal system, the powers to govern the country are divided between the six colonies, or states, and a central government.

Each of these states has their own specific areas of legislative power. The central government is responsible for things like national defense, taxation, postal and telecommunications services, national roads and foreign affairs, as well as governing over Australian territories. (For a complete list see section 51 of the Constitution).

The six individual state governments are responsible for the legislative power of all remaining matters that may occur within their borders. This includes hospitals, schools and education, public transport, and the police force.

Some of the wording in the constitution is such that from time to time it can cause situations where it may appear that both the federal government and the state governments can, if they wish to, claim the authority to make laws over the same or similar areas or matters. When this happens there are special procedures that can be followed to resolve any conflicts or areas of disagreement.

2017 is a significant year because it is the 50th anniversary of the 1967 referendum that resulted in the new laws that recognize Aboriginal Australians as equals.

2017 is also the 25th anniversary of the Mabo ruling. This ruling overturned the earlier law that said all the land of Australia belonged to the British Crown, denying any native ownership, and formally recognized the land rights of the Aboriginal people throughout Australia.

This year is the 20th anniversary of a report called "Bringing Them Home." This report and the protocol of the 10th anniversary of the Northern Territory intervention were set in place so the government could help protect the children living in some of the remote communities who were subject to neglect and violence. All significant milestones in the history of Australia, some are historic and legal; others show the political and cultural relationships between Australia's indigenous and immigrant populations.

During May of 2017, a historic gathering at Uluru of 250 indigenous delegates occurred. They were meeting to decide what form of official constitutional recognition the Aboriginal people should try to seek from the Australian parliament.

Their agenda was to work out the legal and moral framework needed, so they could provide a united front that represented all indigenous Australian people. This was to give a common voice to the Aboriginal nation and ensure the rights of those people were upheld and their interests were accounted for.

Recognition of Australia

Australia's first name was New Holland, but the explorer Matthew Flinders started calling it Terra Australis. The Latin word australis means southern and terra means land. With the support of Governor Macquarie (1810 - 1821), the name was officially changed then abbreviated to Australia.

At a meeting in 1899, the Premiers of the other five Colonies agreed to locate the new federal capital of Australia in New South Wales as this was the most central place for the government to sit. In 1909, the portion of the state of New South Wales where parliament was held was renamed the state of Canberra to house the present day City of Canberra, the Australian Capital.

Australia Day Anniversary

The first official celebration of the English colonization of Australia was held in 1818. This celebration was originally called Foundation Day during the colonial period to mark the landing of the first fleet of ships at Camp Cove on 26th May. Other areas all around Australia also held their annual celebrations of their founding using dates that were relevant or had some significance to their colonies. In 1994, all states and territories of the Commonwealth of Australia decided to change the name of the founding celebration day to Australia Day and all agreed that it would be best to celebrate Australia Day together on the actual day.

Australia Day is, however, for many Indigenous Australians, not a day they feel should be celebrated, but rather a day used to mourn the people, especially the indigenous peoples of Australia who perished and were mistreated making Australia what it is today.

A large number of people now support the view that the Indigenous People of Australia have a genuine grievance, so they support using Australia Day as a day of mourning and protest.

On 26th January 1938 sesquicentennial (150th) celebrations of the founding of Australia saw a group of Aboriginal activists meeting to hold what they called a 'Day of Mourning' conference. This was aimed at securing national citizenship and equal status for all Aborigines. A public referendum on the issue of the Citizenship rights for all Aborigines was finally recognized in 1967. This led to the advanced Aboriginal Movement.

Women's and Indigenous People's Suffrage

Australian women gained the right to vote in 1894, just one year after the women of New Zealand became the first women in the world to win the right to vote. Up until then, men were the only ones who had the right to vote being the head of their household and families. Having the right to vote also made women eligible to stand for election in all public offices, including parliament. And the first one to do just that was Edith Cowan in 1921.

Unfortunately, the wording of the legislation gave full voting rights to all white adults (meaning those over 21 years of age), so it excluded all nonwhites, effectively removing any of the citizen rights of the Aboriginal population. This was a great step forward for Australian women's freedom, but a huge step back for the freedom of the Australian Aboriginal people, as they would not regain their citizenship rights until 1967.

One of Australia's first female political candidates was Catherine Helen Spence; she was also the leader of the Women's Suffrage Movement of South Australia. Although she was never voted into office, her views had a very strong influence on the political and social aspects and people's opinions on women's issues of the time. She was a very active in supporting the rights of all people in Australia including the Aboriginal people and immigrants.

Many other women were very active in exercising their electoral rights. In 1943, Dame Enid Lyons became the first female elected to the House of Representatives, and Dorothy Tangney became Australia's first female senator. More recently, in 1989, Rosemary Follett became the first female head of government in the Australian Capital Territory. Another democratic landmark for Australian women was in 2010 when Julia Gillard became the first female Prime Minister. Also relevant to the suffrage of all Australians is the fact that voting is compulsory in the country, which is a policy that was first introduced in 1924.

Indigenous folks have also been somewhat active in Australia's political life, with Neville Bonner becoming the first indigenous member of the parliament in 1971. In 2010, the House of Representatives also got its first indigenous member by the name of Ken Wyatt.

Chapter 8: Australia's Wars and Their Effects

World War I

Australia was an exciting new nation just starting to grow and prosper with about three million working age men when the First World War began in 1914. The majority of the people living in Australia were either immigrants or the children of immigrants, so they had a good understanding of the threat that this war had on them. Even at such a young age, the Australian nation was a proud one, and the residents ascribed great value to what they had built so far away from Britain. Therefore, for the average Australian man, finding motivation to fight for this new home wasn't difficult.

Many young people at that time were not going to sit back while their country was threatened and their new found liberty was taken from them. A huge number of young men, approximately 420,000, volunteered to join the armed services and fight to preserve their country and their way of life. They were there to fight for their families as well as the future generations. At least that was the general sentiment at the time.

Clearly, there is one question that immediately imposes itself: How exactly, if at all, was Australia really threatened in World

War I. The simple yet somewhat misguided answer would be that it wasn't. However, the Australian position and mindset at that time were much more complicated than that. Although Australia was now a country of its own, the political and cultural ties to Britain were still incredibly strong. Besides, the Commonwealth of Australia was still a dominion of the British Empire at that time. Australians were not forced to fight, far from it, but political pressure was certainly there, although it would have been largely irrelevant given the vigor, morale, and the sheer number of Australian volunteers. Britain was essentially the motherland in the eyes of the vast majority of Aussies, and an actual birthplace to many others.

Furthermore, being such a young country, Australia was yet to build its international reputation and name and, back then, there was hardly any better way of doing that than through war exploits. Australia's commitment to the war effort of its allies would also help break the stigma associated with Australia's convict past. On top of that, Australia could count on its allies in the future if the country was ever to come under attack.

And so, when Britain went to war against Germany on August 4 of 1914, Australia was there to assist. The Australian leadership was unified in its support for the British strife, with both Prime Minister Joseph Cook and Opposition Leader Andrew Fisher vowing that Australia would support Britain whatever it took. Similar enthusiasm engulfed the population, and there was a general excitement to join the fighting.

Although the bulk of Australian involvement was in the Middle East, Australian servicemen were engaged on most other fronts as well. Australia's first notable engagements occurred in September of 1914 in New Guinea. This was when the Australian Naval and Military Expeditionary Force took possession of several German territories in the Pacific, first by landing at Rabaul on the island of New Britain and then by taking the German New Guinea a few days later. Many other nearby islands of the Bismarck Archipelago were captured in the following month. Australia's crowning achievement in the area was the destruction of the German cruiser SMS *Emden* by HMAS *Sydney*.

The bulk of the initial Australian volunteers were shipped to Egypt to assist the British in defending their Middle Eastern colonial interests from the Ottoman Empire, which was a major adversary in the region. The ever-crucial Suez Canal, separating

119

the Sinai Peninsula from Africa, was also under threat and needed to be controlled.

In April of 1915, the Aussie troops set out to participate in the famed Gallipoli Campaign alongside their British, French, and New Zealander allies. The effort to take the Gallipoli Peninsula from the Turks soon turned into a bloody stalemate that went on for the rest of the year. The Ottoman Empire ultimately prevailed, but the casualties on both sides, including the wounded, were in the hundreds of thousands. Among them, there were over 28,000 Australian casualties with close to 9,000 dead.

While battles continued in the Middle East, a great portion of the Australian forces was gradually being moved to Europe's Western Front. Like all the other unfortunate souls on the Western Front, the Aussies too were greeted by an excruciating stalemate in the trenches where every meter of gained ground was paid for in rivers of blood. Bitter fighting continued through 1916, and the following year until the counter-offensives of 1918. The Australian troops memorably distinguished themselves in the capture of Le Hamel, Northern France in July of that year. The push against Germans continued and the Aussies participated all the way until October, while Germany surrendered two months later on November 11. The Ottomans also yielded shortly before that in late October.

The war took the lives of over 60,000 soldiers and injured 156,000, which was a huge loss to the developing country of Australia. With a severe shortage of males in the workforce during the war, the women of Australia took their place and filled all the vacancies to get the jobs done and keep the country moving during and shortly after the war.

As was the case in all major wars of the 20th century, these jobs included various administrative and secretarial positions, as well as the crucial manual labor that kept the war effort going through the production of equipment, munitions, and weapons. The women worked on farms too, but many of them volunteered to fill various logistical roles within the military itself, including the frontlines. Nurses, cooks, translators, drivers, and many other crucial positions were filled by conscionable and patriotic women of Australia.

Hardships at home were far from over after the Treaty of Versailles. With so many men either dead or severely wounded, many women found themselves having to take over many traditionally-male responsibilities in their homes, including putting the food on the table.

When the war ended and the surviving men came home, the Australian government provided them with both the land and funds to establish their farms under an act called the soldier settlement scheme. This was a program that helped many Australian veterans of the Great War and helped the states to populate otherwise uninhabited areas and expand inland. Similar efforts were used to attract selected groups of allied soldiers as well, bringing additional people to Australia. A similar approach was also used after World War II. People felt a new hope and expectancy at the end of the war with the beginning of a boom period called the "Roaring Twenties." People liked to party, dance, and listen to the new styles of music that had been brought back by the returning servicemen. Radio and movie theaters, as well as gramophone players, helped spread the new culture from America and Europe to the new Australia. For the first time, Australia was no longer a backward country, but had all the modern conveniences of the day, including new cars, high fashion clothes, and modern cuisine. Plenty of work was available for everyone who wanted it, including the new immigrants that were arriving constantly.

This trend all came to an abrupt end with the world monetary crash and the Great Depression of 1929. The jobs and finances all dried up as many people fought to survive. Many returned to the land and started growing their own food with the majority barely surviving. The gap between the rich and poor that had reduced over the last decade was more apparent than ever.

Sports and entertainment distracted people from the mundane daily life. The racetrack became very popular thanks to the likes of racehorse Phar Lap, closely followed by cricket which was the national summer game where cricketers like Donald Bradman became superstars.

World War II

Two decades had barely passed, and the world was already set on blowing itself to hell once again. As before, Australia was there, in the thick of things, right next to allied nations from very early on in the war. Australian soldiers volunteered for active duty alongside other members of the commonwealth, such as New Zealanders, Canadians, South Africans, and the British Armed forces. In total, almost a million Australians served in the course of the war.

Aussies saw combat in most of the theaters, including Europe, where they faced off against both Germany and Italy, the Mediterranean, North Africa, as well as Southeast Asia and the Pacific against the Japanese. Unlike in World War I, Australia was directly threatened this time by the forces of Imperial Japan, whose air force reached the mainland and struck parts of northwest Australia. Their submarines also hit Sydney harbor. The war was all too real for every Australian this time, not just the men in the trenches overseas.

Although Australia formally joined in 1939 when Britain and France declared war on Germany after the September 1 invasion of Poland, Aussies didn't start seeing action until the summer of 1940. Australia declared war on the remainder of the Axis powers in Europe in 1940 and against the Empire of Japan in December of 1941.

The first to get in the fight was the Royal Australian Navy, which made contact shortly after war was declared on Italy in June of 1940. The navy struck the enemy in the Mediterranean, where significant damage was inflicted on the Italian naval forces. Notably, Australian HMAS *Sydney*, which was a newer cruiser launched in 1934, participated in the battle at Cape Spada where she helped sink the Italian Bartolomeo Colleoni cruiser. There were also some Australian pilots who participated in the famed Battle of Britain as a part of the Royal Air Force.

The war truly began for the Australian army in 1941 when three divisions were moved to partake in Allied efforts in North Africa and the Mediterranean. Australia's run-ins with the Italians continued to see success, but things took a sour turn for them and the other allies against Germany on Crete, in Greece, and in North Africa. The next significant engagements saw Australian troops join forces with the Allies to invade Syria in early summer of 1941. As Japan entered the war toward late

1941, two of the Australian divisions were moved back to the Pacific to face the threat while one division remained in North Africa to help the British in the decisive Battle of El Alamein, which was a victory in autumn of 1942. The last Australian decision too was shipped out to face the Japanese shortly thereafter.

After attacking the Americans at Pearl Harbor in December of 1941, the battle-hardened Japanese made short work of most of Southeast Asia. By the time they struck the US Navy, the forces of Imperial Japan had been at war with China for over four years, which gave them valuable experience in many aspects of modern warfare. On top of that, Japan was a formidable force by sheer capacity as well, which is why their imperialistic gains in the Pacific were so swift, and they quickly began to threaten the interests of every colonial power in that part of the world. By spring of 1942, a large chunk of the Pacific was under Japanese control.

A swift and crushing defeat was inflicted on the Australians and the British in Singapore, which fell into Japanese hands within a week in February of 1942, costing Australia a whole division in the process. Right after that, the Japanese proceeded to bomb

Darwin in the Northern Territory. Australia began to concentrate as well as expand all of its forces, and the country was starting to prepare for total war as there was a sense of an impending invasion.

However, a wave of relief washed over the Land Down Under the following month when the Japanese war machine started to lose momentum. The now-experienced Australian troops began to pour in from Europe, and Japan began to face defeat, particularly in the crucial Battle of Midway in June. The Americans also vowed to protect Australia by sending material support and reinforcements.

As the Japanese now had their hands full due to the rapidly escalating war with America, the threat of full-blown invasion of Australia began to dissipate. However, Australians weren't about to sit back and let others do their fighting for them. They joined in on the pushback through New Guinea and beyond. Australia took significant initiative here and mounted sophisticated operations, which went well into 1944.

Between Borneo and Bougainville islands, across Indonesia and New Guinea, the Aussies launched offensives against Japanese troops stationed on the many islands in the area in 1944. These sweeping maneuvers began on the islands of Bougainville and New Britain and then gradually progressed westward toward Borneo, where Australian troops were still engaged in combat by the time Japan capitulated in August of 1945.

During the post-1942 struggle against Japan, Australia still had thousands of airmen over European and the Middle Eastern battlefields, where thousands of casualties were suffered in the course of the entire war. Confrontations with German pilots also proved more deadly, even though air combat was commonplace in the Pacific as well.

Overall, around 39,000 Australian soldiers of all branches lost their lives during this devastating war. Particularly dire was the fate of many Australian POWs, most of whom were captured by the Japanese, who used them for forced, hard labor and routinely mistreated them, resulting in around a third of them losing their lives.

Also noteworthy was the role of Australian women in the war effort, which was at an unprecedented level during World War II. The Women's Auxiliary Australian Air Force was formed in early 1941, and females were also being accepted into the navy in various non-combat capacities. Women also formed the Women's Royal Australian Naval Service and the Australian Women's Army Service. These novel formations helped fill up many logistic, administrative, and other posts, which freed up more men to be sent to the frontline. In addition to that, of course, women played a crucial role at home and in the military industry, just like in the Great War.

Many other effects were coming to Australia as a result of the war. When the Second World War ended, Australia accepted thousands of refugees and immigrants. One of the few positive aspects of the war was it created new technologies and methods of manufacturing. Consumers were ready to buy all manner of new products. The Australian economy flourished, and many jobs were available in all different types of industries. People could then afford to purchase their own homes and home ownership reached to over 70%. Interest rates were affordable and wages were relatively high.

This period was a time of real growth, and many new families once again started producing more children with many couples having 3 to 6 children. These children became known as the

Baby Boomers. Now they make up about a third of the workforce. Approximately, 860 baby boomers turn 60 years old every day. Within a few years, they will all be retired.

The Australian government started a program to bring huge amounts of migrant workers into Australia to meet the labor shortages in the country. Between 1945 and 1975, the Australian population grew from 7.5 million people to over 13 million.

Most of those people came from southern Europe and the Mediterranean areas. Their influence is one of the main reasons why Australia has developed in the way it has. These immigrants brought with them new cultural aspects, cuisine, trade, and skills to influence the course of Australia's growth.

One and a half million British people immigrated to Australia on government schemes called "Bring out a Briton." The government subsidized the cost of their immigration and helped them to find work and accommodation. Another scheme called "the Nest Egg Scheme" assisted families that had a small amount saved to start their new lives in Australia. To be exact, those immigrants who had at least 500 pounds in savings were assisted in their travel to Australia with paid expenses to help them retain their full savings and be able to buy a house quickly upon arrival.

Child Migrants and Farm Boys

After the war, many orphaned or neglected children were placed in British welfare institutions because their families either couldn't care for them or just didn't exist anymore. Australia's Minister for Immigration, Arthur Calwell, wanted to bring as many of these children to Australia as possible. Many of these child migrants were sent to training farms or church-run orphanages for long-term care as well as education. Once these children were in Australian orphanages, many were denied any contact with their parents and siblings.

This action was all the result of government programs such as the Fairbridge Farm Movement, which existed prior to the war when the Fairbridge Farm at Molong opened. Sixty children were in this institution before the war, which was a number that Calwell sought to increase. Other similar movements such as the Big Brother movement and various church-organized programs existed. The focus on youth immigration persisted until the 1960s, and thousands of child migrants came to Australia this way.

Problematically, many of these children, with nobody to care for them back home, were forced to go, and the institution that housed and raised them often had great power over them. The institutions were able to shut down attempts by long-lost relatives to get in touch or bring the kids back. Of course, countless reports have surfaced over the years that detailed widespread abuse of all kinds, ranging from harsh discipline to sexual exploitation. This practice, surprisingly, was not questioned for many years, but it came to light in 2009, at which time the Australian government made a formal national apology to the Forgotten Australians including many former child migrants.

Child farm schemes aimed to bring young British boys to settle in Australia as 'farm boys.' When they grew older, they were allowed to nominate their families for assisted passage to come and join them. The success rate of these efforts is highly disputed.

The Balanced Immigration Intake

The government negotiated immigration agreements with European countries because it was concerned about maintaining a balanced intake of immigrants. These agreements were done to ensure the influx of immigrants did not threaten or change Australia's Anglo-Celtic identity and culture. From the early 1950s, Australia had a system of preferred immigrants, also known as the "White Australia" policy. First were the British immigrants, then the Dutch, West Germans, Danes, and other northern or western Europeans. The least preferred immigrants were the southern Europeans. But of those, the ones who most likely qualified were young single men, whose labor would benefit Australian industry.

The Cold War Conflicts and Beyond

The Australian Armed Services have contributed military support to most of the armed conflicts around the world on the side of its allies, Great Britain and the USA, as well as helping the UN Peacekeeping Forces. Since the Second World War, thousands of Australian military personnel have been killed in action.

The first significant Australian involvement in a foreign conflict along with their allies was during the Korean War between 1950 and 1953. As part of the United Nations coalition, some 17,000 Australian troops participated in this war during those years, with over 300 killed in action. After 1953, some Australian officers and other personnel also stayed for a few years with other international observers and peacekeepers.

Although Australia's casualties were relatively low, the Korean War was an important milestone in Australian geopolitics and international relations. The country's international standing was greatly bolstered, and many of Australia's security concerns during the turbulent Cold War years were addressed when Australia, New Zealand, and the US signed the ANZUS Treaty in 1951. In the simplest terms, this treaty guaranteed military cooperation and assistance in the case of an attack on Australia.

Then came the excruciatingly vicious Vietnam War or, to be exact, the portion of it that saw American involvement. Australia's involvement in Vietnam was lengthy, starting in 1962 with the arrival of the Australian Army Training Team Vietnam, also known simply as the Team, and ending in 1973. In the course of the conflict, around 60,000 Australians served in Vietnam, suffering well over 3,000 casualties, 521 of which were killed in action. Similarly to what was going on in America during the 1960s, many Australians were in staunch opposition to the war, resulting in a fair amount of social unrest. As the US escalated its involvement after 1965, so did Australia.

As history remembers all too well, in the early 1970s many realized the communist forces of North Vietnam were making decisive gains and, with the anti-war pressure at home at an all-time high, the Western powers were slowly starting to devise their exit strategy. Most of the Australian troops in the country left Vietnam in early 1973, with only a small unit remaining with the task of providing security for the Australian embassy in

Saigon, which was the capital of South Vietnam at that time. In June of that year, these troops too were withdrawn home.

As Australia continues to foster military ties with the US and the UK, its military has participated in many other conflicts since then, especially during the War on Terror since 2001. In Iraq, Australia participated both in the invasion of 2003 and in the multinational coalition until 2009, though in a limited capacity that resulted in only two casualties. Australia's involvement in the Afghan War since 2001 was more costly, however, leaving 42 soldiers killed in action.

Chapter 9: Immigration and Culture

Immigrating to another country is not an easy decision to make, and the trip itself can be complicated and for some, not easy, specially so for some of the early migrants to Australia. With often overcrowded ships, the requirements of being confined to migrant reception camps and having to live in difficult situations while their immigration paperwork was being assessed and checked made it very difficult.

Bonegilla Camp Victoria was the main immigration processing facility from 1947 to 1971. During the time it was open, over 300,000 people were processed there. The Australian government required all people that were in any type of refugee or immigration facility to attend daily English classes so they would be able to more easily integrate into Australian society. The Australian government has recently been trying to process most immigrants before they arrive in the country make the whole process less stressful.

Since the end of World War Two, Australia has accepted over 870,000 refugees. These have mainly been people who have fled their home countries because of famine, war, or religious persecution.

Not everyone is welcomed into Australia, however. The threat of terrorists and criminals, as well as people with health issues, is the main concern when dealing with both refugees and immigrants. The Australian government is also concerned with allowing people to immigrate to Australia who do not want to assimilate with the rest of the Australian people, because some migrants might have a tendency to adversely affect other Australian citizens. All Australians have a right to live their lives without being physically threatened or otherwise disrupted by people who have different views than they do.

There has also, over the last few years, been a lot of controversy with boat people trying to reach Australia in their own boats. The term "boat people" is used in many parts of the world today to describe refugees fleeing by boat, but it was originally used to refer to South Vietnamese civilians who were desperately evacuating during and after the fall of Saigon in 1975. Many of these unfortunate folks made their way to Australia, Hong Kong, Indonesia, and many other places in the Pacific.

The Australian government has a policy of no boat people being allowed to stop the huge numbers of people trying to enter the country illegally with no identification and no papers. Such policies also serve to dissuade potential boat people for their own safety. Unarmed and packed into small boats, these refugees have traditionally been an easy target for pirates, but many of them would also succumb to hunger, dehydration, and, frequently, drowning.

Even today, thousands of asylum-seeking refugees arrived in Australia by boat from places like Sri Lanka, Iran, and Afghanistan Many more people tried to reach Australia, but perished on the way because of the unsafe and overloaded boats they were traveling on. One incident involved refugees trying to reach Australia, where their boat sunk and resulted in over 70 people missing at sea and 17 deaths.

Every person who immigrates to Australia will have a slightly different experience. What they will experience will depend on where they come from, their level of education, and their ability to speak English. Other factors that can influence what happens to them is their socioeconomic status, their age, gender, and whether or not they have any friends or family connections in Australia.

Australia's growing culture

For much of Australia's short history, the government policies on immigration and accepting refugees were, at both the Commonwealth and State levels, discriminatory against Indigenous Australians and non-Europeans. The White Australia Policy that was in force protected what they called "The Great Australian Way of Life" and kept as well as protected the values of middle class average Australians. In 1967, the Australian people, in a referendum, overwhelmingly made it clear to the government that they did not support any form of discrimination against Indigenous Australians or non-Europeans.

Gough Whitlam, the Prime Minister in 1973, implemented the Government's Universal Immigration Policy that allowed anyone to apply to immigrate to Australia. No restriction was placed on people because of their nationality, color, race gender, ethnic origin, or religion. Anyone could apply and whether he or she was accepted or not would depend entirely on the person and his or her merits.

A points system was introduced in 1979, so a person could assess himself and know if he met the required criteria and would be eligible to apply to immigrate. This proved to be a successful system, and over the next 10 years, over 100,000 people immigrated to Australia from Africa, Asia, and the Pacific Islands.

Australia is now truly an integrated society, a real mixture of different people and cultures from all areas of the world. The rich diversity introduced over the last two hundred years, combined with the rich heritage of the Aboriginal people, has created a unique environment like nowhere else on Earth.

Almost anywhere you look, you see the effect of the contributions made by the different cultures of the migrants and refugees. The shops are overflowing with both contemporary and very modern versions of every type of fashion imaginable. Artists and designers are painting on the great canvas that is becoming tomorrow's Australia. The influences of the different people involved in everyday life often help to improve the quality of life for everyone.

The Australian food industry has developed from a pie and chips at the local pub, to fine dining, cafes, and restaurants that equal anywhere in the world. The different cooking methods and types of foods now grown all around Australia along with the influences that have been introduced have created a new and multilayered Australian cuisine.

Social services such as education, medical, and dental care are world-class and affordable, with the backup of a general government-funded welfare system that caters to all people. Those who genuinely cannot work due to illness, disabled status, or any other life-altering problem are properly cared for by the system, while those who can work are kept on their feet while being given a strong incentive to work and better themselves. These principles largely apply to immigrants in Australia, which is how the country allows people from so many different backgrounds and cultures to come and contribute to Australia's growth.

Immigrant Work

The Australian government has traditionally been mainly interested in obtaining immigrants that were professional, skilled, or semi-skilled. The unskilled immigrants were required to work on some of the government projects since there was no suitable work for them. Often, these projects were located in remote areas, and the immigrants were expected to complete a two-year contract.

One such project was the Snowy Mountains River Scheme, which employed immigrant workers for many years. This enormous hydroelectric and irrigation complex located in southeast Australia took 23 years to build, so it provided opportunities for many manual laborers until 1972. The Snowy Scheme is not a facility but a whole area filled with multiple facilities and structures such as dams, power stations, a pumping station, pipelines, and many tunnels.

Many teachers, nurses, and doctors who successfully immigrated to Australia would take contracts in remote areas as part of their condition of becoming permanent residents or citizens. Over the last 50 years, Australia grew and prospered on immigrant labor, and although the economy has slowed down recently, there will always be many more job vacancies than people to fill them, so Australia will likely need new immigrants for the future.

The types of jobs that are often initially taken by immigrants are home or domestic/helper and home health care jobs, hospitality, and for men there are the coal and steel industries, rail and shipyards, as well as construction of bridges, dams, railways, airports, roads, houses, schools, and offices in many areas including the rapidly expanding suburbs.

The Australian government and the immigration department always give priority to people who have the appropriate skills or are professionals and are able to fill the job vacancies that are available and needed. There are also provisions to accept those immigrants who can provide business expertise or capital for investment that would directly benefit the Australian economy. The Australian government is committed to helping immigrants and is always trying to find new ways to provide the support they need to integrate and become part of the Australian community.

When many skilled or professional migrants first arrive, they find that it can be difficult to have their qualifications and skills recognized. Because of this, many schools and technical colleges offer refresher or update courses to immigrants. Many also offer classes in different languages, including English.

One of the problems facing new immigrants is meeting, getting to know, and becoming accepted by the people in the areas they live and work. Commonly, new immigrants seek out other people from the same or similar background as themselves and form new groups or subcultures without ever mixing or assimilating with the community at large. This occurrence has happened in the major Australian cities such as Sydney, Brisbane, and Melbourne and can lead to self-segregation, which is why refresher courses, English classes, and other assimilatory efforts are so important for new immigrants.

Citizenship

Since Australia was a British colony, everyone born in the colony as well as those who permanently lived there were British subjects. When the Citizenship Act of 1948 was passed, all those people of European descent became Australian citizens. But all non-Europeans were banned from becoming Australian citizens until 1956.

These policies have changed, and all immigrants are now encouraged to apply for Australian Citizenship as soon as possible. The children of Australian citizens, regardless of where they were born, can apply for Australian citizenship by descent. If they were born in another country or if one of their parents is a citizen of another country, they can become citizens of both countries. The law is very clear in Australia that only Australian citizens can be elected to a public office. All candidates must have allegiance only to Australia, so anyone who is a dual citizen or who could be a dual citizen and does not relinquish their other citizenship cannot stand for any public office.

Chapter 10: Australia Today

Australia has changed considerably since the 1970s and '80s when it was mainly a Christian Anglo-Celtic society. Today, it is much more culturally diverse with over half the population or the previous generation born overseas. The awareness of being an immigrant is real for many Australian people.

The intake of migrants has created a new and more complex society that is rich in different cultures and has left many of the old prejudices and animosities behind. Accepting other people's differences, and even welcoming them, has become an important part of life in the new Australia. Many Australian people are now proud to acknowledge their ethnicities and accept that all other people are equal and have equal rights.

Australia has been at the forefront of human rights and humanitarian issues for over a hundred years. In 1850, Australia granted male suffrage and, during the 1890s, female suffrage to its people. Along with New Zealand, it was the first country to give women equal rights and make them equal citizens and created the 40-hour working week and equal pay for men and women. The multicultural democracy has a strong record of protecting its people's civil and political rights.

The government charges the Australian Human Rights Commission t with investigating complaints against all human rights violations as well as promoting human rights through community discussions, education programs, and reporting any abuses. Every Australian's right of free speech, freedom of association, freedom of movement, freedom of religion, and freedom from discrimination is protected. Australia is not only an active member but a founding member of the United Nations. The Universal Declaration of Human Rights that Australia has adopted was partly written by Australians.

Australia has maintained an active and supporting role with many peacekeeping agencies, including operations of the United Nations in different parts of the world to help promote peace efforts and protect human rights.

Australia has had a policy of no boat people since the first Vietnamese refugees arrived in over 50 unseaworthy boats carrying 2000 refugees to Australia in 1976. This policy has caused many humanitarian issues dealing with refugee rights and also the rights of the people of Australia. Until recently, anyone trying to enter Australia illegally has been detained in the immigration processing center on Nauru Island while he or she is being processed.

Currently, Australians have two main political parties, Labor and Liberal, and several minor parties with the balance of power being mostly shared by coalition governments because neither party has been able to obtain a clear majority with enough support to stand alone.

Julia Gillard is the only woman to have been a leader of a major political party in Australia, elected as both the Deputy Prime Minister as well as the Prime Minister. She won the prime minister position after Kevin Rudd resigned because of a vote of "no confidence" in his leadership.

The change in the office came after a shift in the ruling Labor Party. Surprisingly, Rudd had been one of the most popular prime ministers up to that point. The unraveling within the party was largely due to Rudd's concession to the opposition in the senate on the subject of climate change when he abandoned his plan to implement the carbon emissions trading scheme legislation that was in the works. This decision was perceived by his party as a major betrayal, and the perception would have been the same in the public. A significant portion of Kevin Rudd's platform was built upon the notion that climate change was the most pressing issue of our time, and his many supporters wholeheartedly agreed. His choice to back down was, above all, deemed detrimental to his party's chances of winning the coming election, which is the most immediate reason he was forced to resign.

Julia Gillard, as Deputy, was then elected unopposed by her party, becoming the new Prime Minister. In the 2010 election, she led her party to a hung parliament but was able to form a minority government with independent parties. The fallout from

Rudd's fiasco proved too damaging, drastically affecting Labor's performance in the election, which meant that the party lost its majority rule and would have to seek a coalition. Support was found, however, and Gillard managed to form a government with the support of a few independents, including the Greens. Then, after three years and just before the next election, a vote of no confidence caused her to lose her leadership back to Rudd, and she resigned from politics.

Tony Abbott, who was the leader of the Liberal Party, won the 2013 general election and formed the new coalition government. Two years later, his position as PM was challenged by Malcolm Turnbull in a sudden Liberal Party ballot. After winning the vote 55 to 44, Turnbull then became the new PM. Malcolm Turnbull also won the next federal election in July 2016 and still retains the position, but with a low level of public support.

As of November of 2017, the public support for Turnbull and his government hit a new low. The most significant factor causing such low popularity has to be the government's "citizenship crisis." Turnbull's own Deputy PM and six lawmakers were ejected from the parliament when they were discovered to be dual citizens, which is unconstitutional, leaving the government in shambles. Opposing lawmakers took turns threatening to get each other ejected on this basis, and the senate agreed to set a deadline of December 1 for politicians to be forced to publish the birthplaces of their parents. Those who were found to be dual citizens had to renounce their other citizenship in order to remain in the parliament.

Conclusion

One needn't look far past the history of Australia to realize what people are capable of and how far they can get in a short timespan with determination, drive, and by working together toward a common goal. A little over a century has passed since Australia was established as an actual country and fewer than forty years since it achieved full and final independence from the UK. And yet this young country already has a long, eventful, and rich history.

Even more impressive than the country's development is the land of Australia itself along with the fascinating and diverse people that inhabit and continue to build it further. Australian men and women throughout history have come to know the meaning of hard work, dedication, sacrifice, and hardship, and yet they have continuously prevailed even when faced with the harshest of adversities.

However, the people of Australia have also had the bravery and integrity to look within themselves, employ healthy self-criticism, and face their own darknesses when the need arose.

Generations that have come long after the colonial era have, with faith in their country and its future, taken on the monumental task of facing the past head-on and correcting any wrongs that may have been done, no matter how difficult and painful at times. This kind of spirit and mentality made Australia the modern, welcoming, prosperous nation that it is today.

Of course, the giants that sailed the stormy seas and faced the fear of the unknown with a firm belief in the virtues of civilization and exploration have also not been forgotten. And while the methods and the circumstances have changed dramatically in the centuries past, undoubtedly, the same spirit still carries the modern Australian toward the same objective. With all its natural beauty and human potential, Australia can undoubtedly look forward to a bright future on this journey, which has only just begun in the grand scheme of things.

Free Gift

As a way of saying thanks for your purchase, we're offering a special gift that's exclusive to my readers.

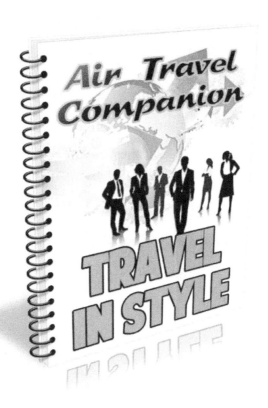

Visit this link below to claim your bonus.

http://dingopublishing.com/bonus/

More Book From Us

Visit our bookstore at: http://www.dingopublishing.com

Below is some of our favorite books:

 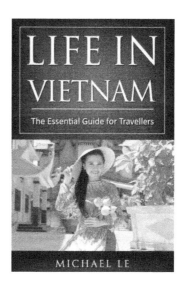

Book excerpt for Japanese Etiquette is available at the end.

SIMPLE, HEALTHY AND DELICIOUS CHIA SEED RECIPES TO LIVE LONGER AND FEEL YOUNGER

CHIA SEEDS Cookbook

Superfoods Every Day

Olivia Green

EASY, HEALTHY AND DELICIOUS KALE RECIPES TO LIVE LONGER AND FEEL YOUNGER

KALE Cookbook

Superfoods Every Day

Olivia Green

RAMEN NOODLES COOKBOOK

The Top 50 Delicious Ramen Recipes To Cook At Home

LINDA NGUYEN

THE TOP 99 DELICIOUS RECIPES TO FIGHT CANCER AND RESTORE YOUR HEALTH

ANTI-CANCER Diet

Olivia Green

INTERMITTENT
FASTING

THE ULTIMATE GUIDE TO BURN FAT
AND BUILD LEAN BODY

JONATHAN SMITH

HIIT

BURN FAT AND BUILD LEAN BODY FASTER WITH
HIGH INTENSITY INTERVAL TRAINING

JOSHUA KING

Bonus Chapter: Japanese Etiquette

Japanese Etiquette by Vincent Miller

Introduction

The Japanese people have an extensive range of customs, rituals, and forms of etiquette for all aspects of their lives. These forms of etiquette are not only interesting for non-Japanese but also open our eyes to the fact that despite the huge strides Japan has made in terms of modern-day advancement in technologies, the age-old customs and traditions are still a deeply-embedded part of their society.

They revere and respect their customs, traditions, and other forms of etiquette and expect people visiting from other countries to do so too. Similarly, the Japanese people are equally respectful of other people's traditions, customs, and etiquette and work hard to understand them so that they don't make a mistake when they visit other countries.

In fact, if you were to travel with any of the Japanese tourist organizations to other countries, the first thing that the guide will talk about is the etiquette expected to be followed there. The Japanese believe that they are ambassadors of their nation and they have to work hard to ensure they leave behind a good impression of their country and its people.

Taking a page out of their etiquette book, it makes a lot of sense to learn about the Japanese forms of etiquette so that we can be prepared to do the right thing at the right time in the right place when we travel to Japan. Moreover, knowing about the culture of another country is a fabulous way of opening our minds and celebrating world differences.

Minding your behavior and your manners reflects a deep sense of discipline and respect for the society and the people you are interacting with. Taking this one step further, the Japanese are a wee bit more attached to etiquette and good behavior than many other countries in the world. As stated earlier, behind the façade of modernity, Japan still is ruled and governed by age-old customs and traditions that are taken very seriously.

The most obvious aspect of these customs and traditions is the etiquette that is unique to Japan and its people. Despite the vast changes in the political, economic and social realms that the country has witnessed over the past hundred years, it has retained its etiquette repertoire in all its ancient splendor and glory.

The modern Japanese take pride in following their forefathers' footsteps in the art of good behavior and pass on their learning to their children too in an effort to keep the traditions alive for many more centuries to come.

This book is written with the intention of giving you insights into the various forms of etiquette the Japanese followed in different social and business settings. Ranging from the correct usage of names and greetings right up to wedding and funeral customs, as much information as possible has been included in this book.

With the etiquette tips in this book, you will be able to handle the expectations of the courteous and polite people of Japan in terms of good behaviour and manners. Most of the people are happy to welcome guests and tourists with open arms and will be even more obliged to do their best to make your stay in their country happy and worthwhile if you show an effort to replicate their etiquette norms and requirements.

163

Chapter 1: The Use of Names

One of the most important elements of Japanese etiquette is to be aware of how to address people and how to use names in different social and business settings.

Addressing People with Respect

San is a commonly used respectful expression that is put at the end of people's names while addressing them. San can be used when using the first name or the last name of the concerned individual. Also, san is used for all people irrespective of marital status or gender.

Sama is a term that is more appropriate in a formal setting and is to be used after the family name. Also, you must remember that you must use san or sama after everyone else's name (whom you wish to show respect to) but not after your own name. Here are some examples of the use of san and sama:

- Smith-san (Mr. Smith)
- Michael-san (Mr. Michael)
- Sandra-san (Ms. Sandra)

- Smith-sama (Mr. Smith again but to be used in a formal setting only)
- Tanaka-sama (Ms. Tanaka)

Another way of respectful address is by using the job title of the person along with his or her name. This works in a scenario where you need to address your superior at work or your teacher at school. For example, you can say Brown-sensei (Brown teacher; sensei is teacher in Japanese) instead of saying Brown-sama. Or bucho-san which is referring to your department head; bucho is head in Japanese.

In business environments, using surname instead of given or first name is more respectful. Use of one's job title instead of their name is also well accepted in Japanese business circles. This subtlety of using surnames instead of first names might come across as a bit stiff for some non-Japanese. However, you must remember that most Japanese are uncomfortable using first names.

However, there are a few Japanese citizens with a lot of exposure to Western cultures that have come to accept being addressed by their first names. Some of them have taken this even further and have created nicknames for themselves, which they embrace happily. You can use these nicknames too along with san or sama depending on the level of formality of the setting.

The final tip here is to remember that you can never go wrong using the surname with the san or sama suffix. For all else, it would be prudent to ask around and then make a sensible choice of addressing the concerned person. The convenience of san cannot be underestimated considering that it is unisex and, therefore, you don't have to worry about how to address people through email especially if the Japanese names are not clearly gender-specific.

Also, if someone is addressing you with the san suffix, accept it as a compliment. That's the intention of the Japanese name-calling etiquette.

Addressing Family and Friends

In Japan, addressing family members and friends also calls for politeness and respect though there is less formality than the use of san or sama. There is a plain form and there is a polite form when it comes to addressing family and friends. Here are a few examples:

- Otto or goshujin – husband
- Tsuma or okusan - wife
- Okoson – child in a polite form and Kodomo – child in a plain form
- Otosan – father in a polite form and Chichi – father in a plain form
- Okāsan – mother in a polite form and haha – mother in a plain form
- musukosan – son in a polite form and musuko – son in a plain form
- musumesan – daughter in a polite form and musume – daughter in a plain form
- otōtosan – older brother in a polite form and ani – older brother in a plain form
- onēsan – older sister in a polite form and ane – older sister in a plain form
- imōtosa – younger sister in a polite form and imōto – younger sister in a plain form
- tomodachi – friend

During conversations, shujin is used to refer to one's own husband and otto is used to refer to someone else's husband. Tsuma is used to refer to one's own wife and kanai is used to refer to someone else's wife

Here's the trick when it comes to using the plain form or the polite form. If you are addressing an older member of the

167

family, then you must use the polite form. When addressing the younger members of the family (spouse also comes in the category), you can use the plain form. To get this right, you must also know the difference between referring to someone and addressing someone.

Referring to someone means you are not talking to the person but are referring to him or her in a conversation with someone else. Addressing someone, on the other hand, is talking to the person directly.

Commonly Used Japanese Expressions

While we are at this, let me also give you the top five commonly used expressions in Japanese conversations:

Yatta – I did it! – You can use this term whenever you have accomplished or been offered a great job or have won something. All these occasions can be classified under the 'Yatta' category.

Honto – Really? – This expression is used to let the person speaking to you know that you are listening to what is being said.

Â, SÔ DESU KA – I see – Also, a conversational bit of phraseology letting your partner (the one who is talking to you) know you are getting what is being said. A nod invariably accompanies this expression.

Mochiron – of course! – An expression of confidence

Zenzen – not at all – a phrase of emphatic denial (in a polite way) used for situations such as when someone asks you, "Am I disturbing you?" and you politely say, "zenzen."

Chapter 2: Greetings and Body Language Etiquette

There are many ways of greeting people when you meet them. This chapter is dedicated to these Japanese greeting methods.

Bowing

Bowing, or bending at the waist level, is a form of appreciation and respect shown by the person who is bowing to the person who is being bowed to. Bowing is a common form of greeting used along with:

- Good morning - ohayo gozaimasu
- Hello, good afternoon - konnichi wa
- With words of apology or gratitude (arigato)

There are three types of bows depending on how deep the waist is bent. These three types include:

The casual bow (eshaku bow)

Bending at a 15-degree angle, the casual bow also entails a slight tipping of the head. The eshaku bow is used when casual greetings are passed between people or when you pass someone belonging to a higher social status. Casual greetings in the form of good morning or good afternoon or thank you are sufficient by themselves. Yet, when used along with the eshaku bow makes the greeting more heartfelt.

The business bow (keirei bow)

This bow entails bending your torso at 30 degrees and is used when entering and/or leaving a meeting or conference or while greeting customers.

Deep bow (saikeirei bow)

This is the politest form of bowing in Japan and entails lowering the torso by 45 degrees. It is used to express very deep feelings of regret (apology) or gratitude.

Clasping Hands (Gassho)

Bringing both the palms together and clasping them in front of the chest is referred to as gassho. This form of greeting has its origins in Buddhism. Today, it is used before starting a meal and after finishing the meal along with the word, 'itadakimasu.' The word, 'itadakimasu,' means to receive or to accept an item or gift. It expresses gratitude for the food and for the person(s) who prepared the meal.

Bye-Bye

While 'sayonara' is the Japanese word for saying goodbye, the phrase 'bye-bye;' is also commonly used in the country. There is a subtle difference in the way the hand gesture works with sayonara. While in the West, you would open and close your palm as you lift your hand, in Japan, your open palms are waved from left to right and back. The hand is lifted high above your head so that the other person can see it and then the open palms are waved from left to right and back in a broad arch. The eshaku bow is also used commonly while saying bye-bye.

Shaking Hands

Although bowing is the more appropriate Japanese form of greeting, the handshake has come to be an accepted form of greeting, especially in a business setting. However, it is important to note that the handshake of the Japanese is far limper than the 'firm handshake' of the Western culture. This is easy to understand considering that the Japanese culture does not allow for too much physical contact, especially in public.

Body Language Etiquette

Nodding is an important gesture in Japan. When you are talking to someone, it is important that you nod often to imply comprehension. Your nod is telling the speaker that you are listening to him or her, and you are understanding what the person is trying to say.

Silence is an accepted form of nonverbal communication. There is no need to chatter merely to keep a conversation going. Silence is, in fact, an expected means of communication. Talk only when addressed or when it is your turn to do so.

Standing very close to a Japanese person is considered rude and uncomfortable. Avoid touching as much as possible except for that first handshake (the bow is a better option).

Making prolonged eye contact when talking to someone is also considered rude in Japanese culture.

Hugging, shoulder slapping, and other forms of physical contact are also to be avoided, especially in public. The Japanese frown on any outward show of affection of any kind.

Using your forefinger to beckon is disallowed. The Japanese way of beckoning calls for extending your right arm and bending the wrist in the downward direction. You are not allowed to beckon any person older than or senior to you.

How to Sit Correctly

Sitting in Japanese style calls for sitting on the floor and in an upright position. Even meals are had while sitting on the floor with low tables for the food. For tea ceremonies, it is mandatory to sit on the floor.

Both genders use the kneeling, or the seiza, posture to sit in a formal environment. It can get uncomfortable after some time for people (especially Westerners) who are not used to this way of sitting. In modern times, foreigners are exempted from sitting on the floor. In fact, many modern Japanese also find it difficult to sit like this for long. In casual environments, it is common to see men sitting cross-legged and women sitting with both their legs to one side.

If you are sitting on a chair, you are expected to sit with both your feet firmly placed on the ground. You cannot cross your legs or place your ankle on the knee while sitting on the chair.

The seating order works something like this: the most important person (usually the customer or the guest) is furthest away from the door. The place that is farthest away from the door is considered to be the good side in Japanese culture.

If there is a tokonoma (an alcove decorated with a hanging scroll accompanied by a flower arrangement), then the guest is usually placed in front of it. The least important person or the host takes the place closest to the door.

Also, in a business environment, all the people from the same company are seated on the same side of the table. When you visit Japanese businesses, it is common for the receptionist to show you your seat. If you don't see this happening, it might be prudent to ask before taking a seat.

Chapter 3: Bathing Etiquette (Onsen)

Bathing has two connotations in Japanese culture. While one meaning is what non-Japanese people are most familiar with is to cleanse the body, the second connotation is to use bathing as a means of relaxation. Bathing for the second reason is a great cultural experience in Japan. Initially, you might feel intimidated and, perhaps, even a bit shy. But once you get used to the joys of the Japanese bathing experience, it can become an addiction.

Like all things in Japan, using the public baths (for relaxation purposes) is replete with behaviours of etiquette everyone is expected to follow. The baths, or onsens, dot the entire landscape of the country and you will find many as you travel through Japan. Not following bathing etiquette is deeply frowned upon. So, here are the etiquette steps you should be aware of:

Entrance to the Baths

The entrances to most of the baths are covered with 'noren' curtains that act like fabric dividers for privacy. There are separate baths for men and women. Women get the blue noren and the men get the red noren.

It is important that you check for the right bath before entering. Quite often, the baths are switched which means what was the women's in the morning could become men's in the evening and vice versa. So, please check carefully and ensure you open the right noren.

Changing Rooms

These rooms are attached to the onsens and are usually equipped with locker facilities and/or baskets for your clothes. There are some onsens that also have hair dryers, chairs, and other facilities here. It is important to check if the onsen you are visiting has toilet facilities or else you must visit the toilet before entering the bath.

The changing room is where you will take off all your clothes and put them in your designated basket or locker. Valuables, jewelry, accessories and spectacles should also be removed and placed here. Slippers are not usually allowed inside onsens. There will be a place outside earmarked for footwear.

Washrooms

Washrooms are different from the relaxing bathing areas (in the form of tubs or hot springs). You must first cleanse your body in the washroom. Rinse yourself thoroughly to ensure no oil, shampoo, or soap is still lingering on your body. Only then; can you step into the bath. The bathing area is only for soaking and relaxing.

The following steps will help you through the process of bathing in Japanese onsens while ensuring no breach of etiquette occurs:

- Clothes have to be removed in the changing rooms
- Cleanse, rinse, and wash your body
- Get into the bath and soak and enjoy yourself

Tips for Bathing Etiquette

Before

Follow the red and blue noren curtains and ensure you enter the bath meant for your gender. Visit the toilet before you get inside the bath. Drink sufficient water to prevent the risk of dehydration.

Remove clothes, valuables, and other accessories in the changing room and place in your designated locker/basket. Cleanse and rinse your body in the washing rooms. Tie up your hair if it is very long. A modesty towel is usually supplied to cover yourself when you move between the bathing area and the washing area. Excessive intake of food and alcohol should be avoided before the bathing ritual.

During

Use of the modesty towels also has etiquette to follow. Men cover their private parts with them, and the women cover themselves from the breasts downward to the genitals. As soon as they enter the bath, the towels are moved up to cover their heads. When they come out of the bath, the towels from the head position move to the prvious position again.

As the areas surrounding the bath will be wet and slippery, it is essential that you walk carefully. Rinsing and washing your body is not allowed in the bathing area. It is restricted to the washing areas only. There are options where you can do a quick rinse using the water from the bath. However, you can do this only by dipping some water into a washing bowl and then slowly rinse and cleanse yourself OUTSIDE the bath and not inside. Only when you are clean can you enter the bath.

Some onsens may not have showers in the washroom. In such places, buckets will be provided. If there is no separate supply of water for the washrooms, you can dip the bucket (or wash bowl) and fill it with water from the tub itself. Some places have stools with water faucets you can use to cleanse yourself. Please check if the facility you are visiting supplies soap and towels or else

181

you might have to carry your own. Remember to return the wash bowl/bucket back to where you took it from so that others can use it.

Do not put your towel, soap, shampoo, or anything else inside the tub. Ensure your towel is on your head or near the side of the bath. You are free to get in and out of the bath any number of times as you wish. Most of the places do not allow for wearing swimming suits. No smoking or washing clothes in the wash area.

After

Don't forget to retrieve your valuables and other items from the changing rooms. Drinking something after your soak is good for rehydration. Some onsens have massaging and relaxing rooms where bathers sit or sleep and relax after the soak. Wet towels should not be placed on the floors. Put them in the designated place.

Some More Important Tips

- Tattooed people are not allowed in some onsens. Please check before you go.

- Menstruating women or infants are not allowed in onsens.

While these are some of the basic etiquette tips for bathing in Japan, once you get used to them, you will find it great to visit onsens as often as you can because they are truly relaxing.

************** End of Sample Chapters**************

Japanese Etiquette by Vincent Miller

Learn more at:

http://dingopublishing.com/book/japanese-etiquette/

Thanks again for purchasing this book.

We hope you enjoy it

Don't forget to claim your free bonus:

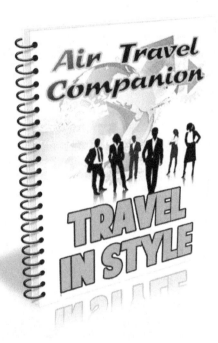

Visit this link below to claim your bonus:

http://dingopublishing.com/bonus/

Made in the USA
Las Vegas, NV
13 May 2023

72016219R00111